STRUCTURED GROUPS FOR NON-TRADITIONAL COLLEGE STUDENTS

Non-cognitive Assessment and Strategies

Siu-Man Raymond Ting

University Press of America,® Inc.
Lanham · Boulder · New York · Toronto · Plymouth, UK

Copyright © 2008 by
University Press of America,® Inc.
4501 Forbes Boulevard
Suite 200
Lanham, Maryland 20706
UPA Acquisitions Department (301) 459-3366

Estover Road
Plymouth PL6 7PY
United Kingdom

All rights reserved
Printed in the United States of America
British Library Cataloging in Publication Information Available

Library of Congress Control Number: 2007940648
ISBN-13: 978-0-7618-3975-0 (paperback : alk. paper)
ISBN-10: 0-7618-3975-5 (paperback : alk. paper)

∞™ The paper used in this publication meets the minimum
requirements of American National Standard for Information
Sciences—Permanence of Paper for Printed Library Materials,
ANSI Z39.48—1984

To my wife, Elsa,
who has supported and loved me
for the past 20 years,
and to my son Nathaniel

and

to the teachers and the mentors
who have inspired
and nurtured me tirelessly

Contents

Foreword	vii
Preface	ix
1. College Student Retention	1
2. Non-Traditional Students, First Year Programs, and Services	13
3. The ExCEL Group—Developmental Structured Groups, Theories, and Strategies	19
4. Establishing the ExCEL Group	33
5. Non-Cognitive Assessment for Group Members	39
6. ExCEL Group Process—Study Skills	47
7. ExCEL Group Process—Non-Cognitive Topics	55
8. Group Evaluation	67
9. Research Studies	71
10. What's Next?	79
Appendix	85
Bibliography	95
Subject Index	105
About the Author	109

Foreword

Professor Ting has written a book that provides a useful strategy for working with nontraditional students through the use of structured groups. The book contains specific examples and strategies that can be applied in a variety of contexts. While other authors have addressed some of these same issues, Professor Ting has based his concepts and examples on research. By discussing his ideas in the context of the work on noncognitive variables, he accomplishes something that most do not; he combines scholarship with practical suggestions and experience. This book should be valuable for anyone who is working with nontraditional students as a teacher, counselor, student service professional, or researcher. The content provided in this book has the possibility of moving the whole field of noncognitive variable research and application to another level. All fields need this from time to time to remind us of the promise of higher education and the role of scholarship. Aside from its use by professionals, the book should result in benefits to many students who might otherwise struggle with the difficult issues that restrict their development.

William E. Sedlacek
Emeritus Professor
University of Maryland-College Park

Preface

Student retention has recently been a focus for new intervention programs and research studies in higher education. There are many books on first-year programs or services aiming to improve student performance and retention; however, comparatively little has been written using a group approach. This book, based on repeated empirical studies of different programs and services, proposes using a group approach with non-cognitive strategies to enhance student development. Specifically, the group aims to assist students in adjustment to the college environment and enhancement of their academic performance, and to increase student retention.

This book is designed to inform higher education professionals—particularly those who work with first-year university students in venues such as orientation, academic advising, counseling centers, first-year programs/classes, housing and multicultural student services—of group-based designs that they can put into practice. Professionals in other functions, such as admissions and financial aid, may also find the book useful. The book covers: (a) the challenges facing university students, particularly during the freshman year; (b) the structured group model; (c) group strategies derived from the non-cognitive approach; (d) groups skills and processes for structured groups; (e) topics and activities for the structured group; (f) case studies of the structured group from universities; (g) evaluation for group outcomes; (h) outcomes from related empirical studies; (h) guidelines for developing the group; and (i) implications for future development of support programs in higher education.

The book begins by addressing the problem of college student retention and how higher education seeks to provide different programs/services for these needs. Then it presents the theory of the Non-Cognitive Model (Sedlacek, 2004). Next, the non-cognitive strategies are applied in the Excellent Commitment and Effective Learning (ExCEL) group, a developmental structured group approach for first year college students, particularly those who are non-traditional, academically underprepared or at-risk. Applications in multicultural settings are addressed through discussion of student cases from different ethnic/cultural backgrounds. The theory and concepts of developmental structured groups are then reviewed, followed by basic group skills for the ExCEL program, including establishing a group, publicizing and recruiting members, screening and selecting members (including preliminary meeting), and preparing members for group sessions. Next, based on the non-cognitive model, the group content and process is discussed, including examples of group materials, activities and homework. Research studies on the ExCEL group which support its pedagogical value are included at this point. Finally, practical and research issues are discussed in the last chapter, including challenges and opportunities for the future.

Siu-Man Raymond Ting
Raleigh, North Carolina
July, 2007

Chapter 1:
College Student Retention

The United States clearly suffers from a disparity between ethnic majorities and minorities in terms of college enrollment and degree completion. For example, in 2000, the breakdown of U.S. undergraduate enrollment by ethnicity was: Caucasian, non-Hispanic [69.3%], African American [11.6%], Hispanic [9.6%]; Asian American [6.4%], Native American/Alaskan Native [1.0%], foreign students [2.3%] (Chronicle of Higher Education, 2002). In sciences and engineering, the gap in bachelor's degree completion in 2001 was larger: 67.7 % Caucasians, 8.8% Asians, and 15.8% underrepresented minorities (8.1% African Americans, 7.0% Hispanics, and 0.7% Native Americans), only a slight increase of 1.8% compared to 1992 (National Science Foundation, 2004).

By 2015, African Americans are projected to make up 14.5% of the total 18-to-24-year-old population, but they are also projected to account for only 11.9% of that age college population (Carnevale & Fry, 2000). Similarly, Hispanics will be 18.9% of all youth in the traditional college-age bracket, but will account for only 13.1% of 18-to-24-year-old undergraduates. In other words, our university campuses will be missing 250,000 African American and 550,000 Hispanic undergraduates.

A study by the Southern Education Foundation (SEF) revealed that African Americans' participation in higher education in 19 southern states in the past twenty years has barely budged. Since setting a record of 15% of first-time full-time freshmen undergraduates at public four-year institutions in 1976, African Americans accounted for 17% in 1996. Historically, these 19 states once operated racially separate college systems.

Among these African American students, only 12.1% studied at traditionally European American dominated universities. An even smaller portion of only 8.6% of the freshman attended flagship southern state universities. In fact, nine of the nineteen states reported a declined percentage of African American freshmen classes between 1991 and 1996.

Like many other studies, the SEF study also found that African Americans are more likely than European Americans to drop out from college. For example, only about two-thirds of the African American freshmen graduated from college within six years. That means about one-third of them did not complete a degree or dropped out.

The SEF study cited a few possible reasons for comparatively low African American enrollment and dropping out. First, a major barrier is admission standards based on standardized test scores such as the SAT. It was found that African Americans have comparatively lower SAT scores than European Americans. Since major institutions use the SAT as their main admissions criterion, the public flagship institutions have been very inaccessible for the African American students.

Admission Criteria: Standardized Test Scores

The SEF study echoes the criticism of SAT scores being used as the sole/major factor for college admissions. SAT scores have been widely criticized as major barriers to the enrollment of students from diverse backgrounds. One explanation for the comparatively low admission and increased attrition of African American students in four-year colleges is that the SAT—the prevailing tool for determining which African Americans are admitted to college in the first place—does not accurately reflect their aptitude for success in college (Ancis & Sedlacek, 1997; Baron & Norman, 1992; Bowen & Bok, 1998; Fleming, 1984; Sedlacek, 1998). The main reason: minority students, on average, consistently score far lower than white students. Others questioned the validity of the relationship between SAT scores and students' grades in college, hence the validity of its use as admission criteria. In fact, the SAT was not originally developed for admissions, but rather for the comparison and measurement of the mathematical and verbal skills of a homogenous population and only with the aim of predicting their first-year college performance (The College Board, 1988; 1996).

As it has turned out, conflicting results regarding the predictability of academic performance using SAT scores have been found. The College Board studies show that SAT scores can moderately predict students' academic performance, with correlation coefficients of .3 to .4 (Burton & Ramist, 2001; Hezlett, Kuncel, Vey, Ahart, Ones, Campbell, & Camara, 2001). Correlation coefficient is a score representing the relationship between a variable and students' GPAs. A score of 1.0 represents a perfect correlation. Researchers use another number called the "explained variance" in conjunction with the correlation coefficient. This figure is expressed as a percentage and explains the differences between any two students' GPAs. To arrive at this figure, the correlation coefficient is squared. Hence the SAT score alone represents roughly 9% to 16% of the variance in students' GPAs in the above studies. To put it another way, 84% to 91% of the variance is explained by factors other than the SAT. For high school GPA, the explained variance is about 16% to 25% (Zwick, 2002). In other words, SAT scores are not better than high school GPAs at predicting college students' grades.

On the contrary, many other studies found little or no relationship between SAT scores and students' performance and retention (Ancis & Sedlacek, 1997; Baron & Norman, 1992; Ting, 2000b; Tracey & Sedlacek, 1987). These studies show that SAT scores could somewhat predict students' academic performance in the first year, *but not afterward*. In addition, SAT scores have been found to have less predictive power for the performance of ethnic minorities than for Whites (Hood, 1992; Ting, 2000a; Ting & Robinson, 1998; Tracey & Sedlacek, 1984, 1985; 1987). SAT scores have also been more strongly correlated with the academic performance of regularly admitted students than those students who did not meet normal admission criteria (Houston, 1980; Ting, 1997a; Westbrook & Sedlacek, 1991; White & Sedlacek, 1986). The relationship between standardized test scores and college graduation is also inconsistent, with several studies reporting only moderate correlation (Adelman, 1999; Manski & Wise,

1983). Moreover, standardized test scores have also been found to be ineffective in explaining student attrition (Baron & Norman, 1992; Sowa, Thompson, & Bennet, 1989; Ting, 1997a; Ting & Robinson, 1998; Tracey & Sedlacek, 1984; 1985). Therefore, the validity of using SAT scores for college admissions is still controversial.

In response to conflicting opinions about the SAT's efficacy as a college performance predictor, close to 300 colleges and universities have abandoned the use of SAT-I scores as the sole or major factor in admissions, some to the point of eliminating the requirement altogether. For example, the University of California System, recognized nationally as one of the best and most forward-thinking institutions in public higher education, has adopted a comprehensive review policy for undergraduate applicants. In addition to standardized test scores such as SAT-I, other factors now include likely contribution to the institution, diversity in personal background and experience, leadership, motivation, concern for others and for the community, and non-academic achievements. It is important to note that "no single attribute or characteristic guarantees the admission of any applicant." (University of Berkeley, 2003). In the first year that UC-Berkeley relied less on SAT scores, officials found that 25 % of the admissions decisions were different than they would have been if the old procedure had been in place (Gose & Selingo, 2001). After adopting this comprehensive review, in 2002, UCLA and UC-San Diego each experienced increases in minority students admitted: jumping to 17% from 15.6% and to14.2% from 11.1%, respectively (Hebel, 2002). Also, the number of applicants and admitted students coming from disadvantaged backgrounds – those from low-income families, who are first-generation students, or who attended a particularly challenged high school – increased at UCLA and UC –San Diego. Meanwhile, the UC System's faculty report concluded that the academic preparation of the incoming classes at those campuses remained stable.

Other non-public colleges (e.g. Mount Holyoke College, Bates College, and Muhlenberg College) do not require their applicants to submit their standardized test scores, such as SAT-I. In fact, over 281 colleges and universities have abandoned the use of SAT-I scores as the sole or major factor in admissions (National Center for Fair and Open Testing, 2000). Simultaneously, many universities are aggressively trying to recruit and retain more students of color, particularly Blacks and Hispanics. Thirteen top colleges, including Harvard University, the Massachusetts Institute of Technology, and the University of Michigan at Ann Arbor, have participated in a study to determine if state exams already given to high-school students may one day be used in college admissions (Gose & Selingo, 2001). Among the new efforts in recruiting more diverse students, there is a common search for non-cognitive or additional criteria for admissions. The common element among these efforts is the search for criteria that will provide a comprehensive evaluation of the university applicant. Factors now being considered include high school GPA or class rank, high school coursework, leadership experience, community services, special talents, and the presence of a disadvantaged background. In some ways, a part of these new criteria were founded in related theories/literature or were documented in scientific studies in some way.

Financial Aid

Second to the SAT admission requirement, lack of need-based financial aid is another reason for such low minority college enrollment. The aforementioned SEF study found that roughly one-third of all university financial aid was merit-based in the Southern U.S. This figure is about 10 times the percentage of aid being distributed on a non-need basis in the 31 other states. However, in 12 of the 19 southern states, at least 30% of all African American families had incomes under $10,000; compared to the financial need in Southern families, the unmatched need is evident.

Other studies show that financial aid was a factor for college enrollment (Astin, 1997). For example, financial aid in the form of grant from a college was found to be positively related to college student development. Merit-based scholarships were related to intellectual self-esteem and increased interests in artistic majors such as music or art. Astin (1997) reported that institutional aids had a stronger link to student retention than federal or state grants. Astin thought that institutional aids are perceived as a form of special recognition for the student's individual talent and potential, while federal or state aids are seen as an entitlement based on financial need. As a consequence, students receiving institutional aid are more likely to continue to be successful and be persistence in their studies.

However, having need-based aid was found to have negative effects on college GPAs (Astin, 1997). It is clear that factors for student retention are complicated. One possible explanation is that financial aid is a necessary factor for college enrollment, but this alone is not a sufficient condition. Other factors discussed here previously should be considered, such as academic background and preparation, psychosocial development and readiness for college.

Role Models/Mentors

Literature shows that many students of color lack role models or mentors. The SEF report observes that African American faculty members, "essential for providing role models and mentoring," were concentrated mainly at community colleges and Historically Black Concentrated Universities (HBCUs). For instance, in Mississippi, 87% of African American faculty was at community and HBCUs. In North Carolina and Maryland, that number was 80% and 66% respectively.

To cope with the challenge of admitting students from diverse backgrounds, promising practices have emerged in some states, including Florida and Georgia. Both states have adopted a new admission policy of admitting students of a certain percentile rank in high school, for example top 10 %. Early research findings reveal that academic achievement has not dropped and the race composition has expanded.

In Florida, first, the state admits the top 90th percentile of applicants from public high schools into their state universities; however, such an arbitrary admission figure was not well-considered. Admissions officers should have consulted school districts and other related constituents before establishing their new admissions policies. There were insufficient seats for all top 10% students. Thus, Florida scaled back from the top 10% to the top 5% of high school students.

Theories of Student Retention

Major theories were developed to explain college performance, including involvement theory, a student departure model and a non-cognitive variables model.

Involvement Theory

Astin (1984) suggested that student involvement was the most important predictor for student retention: "Student involvement refers to the amount of physical and psychological energy that the student devotes to the academic experience" (Astin, 1984, p. 297). Astin found specific factors that were related to student's involvement in academics. One of the factors was the level of perceived fit between the student and institution. Astin (1984) states," it is easier to become involved when one can identify with the college environment" (p. 303).

Another factor was peer group relationship and access to faculty. Astin proposed that frequent interaction with faculty is related to student's satisfaction with college more than any other type of involvement; therefore, universities are encouraged to develop environment conducive to student and faculty interaction and to facilitate students to be actively involved in their studies and campus activities. Other involvement factors include time allocation, courses taken, specific learning experiences, specific pedagogical experiences, student peers, work, and use of leisure time (Astin, 1997). Such factors are usually not a part of assessment of standardized tests, but studies show that these factors are related to academic performance and retention (Astin, 1997).

Student Departure Model

Tinto (1975; 1987; 1993) suggested that college experiences, particularly in the first year of study, can be understood as a cultural adjustment process. He states that college is " a longitudinal process of interactions between the individual and the academic and social systems of the college during which a person's experiences in those systems . . . continually modify his (sic) goal and institutional commitments in the ways which lead to persistence and/or to varying forms of dropout (1975, p. 94). Tinto believes that college freshmen go through a few stages in the first year of study: separation from original community, transition into a new campus, and incorporation into academic and social life of the new campus.

In his model, Tinto proposed that an individual's pre-entry attributes determines his or her goals/commitment, which in turn affect the student's experience on a university campus and, indirectly, how he or she integrates into academic and social life. As a result, an individual will evaluate their goals and commitment in order to make a decision to persist or to leave. In the beginning, pre-entry attributes comprise individual attributes, family background, and precollege experiences. Individual attributes include age, gender, race, intelligence, aspirations, and values. Family background refers to socio-economic status, living environment, parent's education level, and ethnic and cultural influences. Precollege experiences include characteristics of the high school, academic performance, course work, and peer development.

Tinto proposed that student persistence or withdrawal was determined by the level of student integration into academic and/or social systems of the new college/university. Academic integration can be understood as having structural and normative dimensions. Structural dimensions are the formal structure of academics, such as academic standards, and are measured by academic performance, such as grades. Normative dimensions refer to identification with the normative structure of the academic system as measured by student's intellectual development. Normative integration reflects how well the individual's intellectual development matches with the intellectual environment and status of the campus. For example, a collegiate student will appreciate the studying atmosphere of a research-intensive university while a foreclosed student may not have a clear goal and can feel bored and difficult on the same campus.

Social integration is a match between the individual student and the social system. Tinto believes that peer groups and relationships, extra curricular activities, and interaction with faculty and professional staff are important elements of social integration. For example, a student needs to be accepted into a group either at the residence hall, in a class, or in a student club.

The student's decision to stay on or leave a campus—a decision that Tinto warns may be made early, even during the first semester—is determined by his or her level of academic and social integration (Tinto, 1993). Initial commitments affect student's subsequent level of commitment; a high level of social integration may compensate for low levels of academic integration, and vice versa.

Research studies show that many of Tinto's concepts are valid (Braxton, Sullivan & Johnston, 1997; Milem & Berger, 1998), while others queried the validity of the conceptual framework based on academic and social integration (Attinasi, 1992; Biggs, Torres, & Washington, 1998; Tierney, 1992). These scholars argue that, besides the factors upon which Tinto's work focuses, other factors such as economic, psychological and organization factors are also found to be important in student retention.

Non-Cognitive Model

The discourse surrounding the quest for a scientifically-based approach to assessing the aptitude for success in college—the use of noncognitive variables—

has been parsimonious and has therefore accumulated numerous research findings (Sedlacek, 2004). In general, the non-cognitive variables produced variances similar to or better than standardized test scores in estimating grades for different student groups and in predicting student retention (Arbona & Novy, 1990; Boyer & Sedlacek, 1988; Fuertes, Sedlacek & Liu, 1994, Fuertes & Sedlacek, 1995; Hood, 1992; Sedlacek & Adams-Gaston, 1992; Ting, 1997a, Ting, 1998, Ting, 2000a, Ting 2000c ; Tracey & Sedlacek, 1984, 1985, 1987; White & Sedlacek, 1986).

The Noncognitive Questionnaire (NCQ; Tracey & Sedlacek, 1984) has been developed to assess the level and development of non-cognitive dimensions of students. It is a multiple-choice survey combined with three open-ended items to assess pre-college experience, motivation and college expectations for the sake of alternative admissions criteria. Over the past 20 years, numerous research studies have reinforced the power of this model.

Academic performance and performance on achievement tests such as the SAT or ACT are thought to be closely related to intelligence (Sedlacek, 1996; Sternberg, 1993; Ting & Robinson, 1998). Sternberg (1993) found confusion in professional literature between intelligence and intelligent behavior. He wrote,

> What constitutes intelligent behavior may differ from one environmental context to another...intelligence refers to differences in what constitutes intelligent behavior in one group versus another. But the mental processes necessary to generate these diverse behaviors may actually be the same. Intelligence, I argue, has a common core of mental processes that manifests itself behaviorally in different ways in different contexts. For example, the ability to learn is important in any environmental context, but what is learned, both in terms of declarative and procedural knowledge, may differ radically from one environmental context to another. Thus, both the average American and the average Kpelle [an ethnic tribe] need to learn to sort objects, but the learned kinds of rules, according to which they sort in various situations (what constitutes intelligent behavior) may differ. (p. 103)

Sternberg believes that human intelligence can be understood from a new perspective, in addition to the traditional cognitive approach. In his book, *Another Intelligence,* he proposed beyond our understanding of human intelligence based on clinical and cognitive studies, which emphasize mostly the brain development and functioning, there is another domain of intelligence from a psychosocial and environmental perspective. Sternberg (1993) defines intelligence as the ability to adapt to, shape, and select the environmental context, which includes physical, biological and cultural aspects. His theory of intelligence offers a conceptual framework suggesting that three types of intelligence exist (Sternberg, 1985). *Componential intelligence* is defined as the ability to interpret information in a structured and well-defined context. Among the types of intelligence, an individual needs only componential intelligence to interpret information in standardized aptitude tests such as the SAT. Sternberg assumes humans are influenced by environment and psychosocial development. *Contextual intelligence* refers to instrumental acts of advising, consulting, and perhaps influencing others through advice. Contextual intelligence is assessed in the Non-Cognitive Model through the constructs of a self-appraisal system, a supporting person and self-confidence. *Experiential intelligence* is the ability to see issues from different points of view, interpret information in changing contexts, and to resolve practical problems. This facet of Sternberg's description of intelligence is assessed in the Non-Cognitive Model through the constructs of knowledge acquired in a field, community service, leadership experience, extra-curricular activities, and demonstrated ability to live in a multicultural society.

The traditional higher education admissions system tends to concentrate on standardized tests, which represent componential intelligence, the ability to interpret information in a structured and well-defined context. Therefore, the aptitudes of students with well-developed contextual and experiential intelligence, particularly those from non-traditional backgrounds, may be grossly underrated. Even assuming some mental processes may be common across environmental contexts, the ability, motivation, or tendency to apply these processes across contexts may not be equal. As a result, different college students may not appear equal in their intelligent behaviors. Yet, our higher education institutions persist in using standardized test scores and previous grades to predict how well prospective students will learn.

Sedlacek's (2004) non-cognitive variable model captures the essence of Sternberg's intelligence theory by measuring the attributes of experiential and contextual intelligence—facets of intelligence that are almost completely ignored by grades and standardized tests. However, other dimensions of the learning process, including components of experiential intelligence such as students' studying styles, ways of learning, and skills at resolving practical problems, can be explored further. Motivation to study, involvement in college life, and responses to a different physical and cultural environment have generated new, important non-cognitive domains and items for the NCQ. For example, Ting and Robinson (1998) found that socio-economic background, planned working hours, financial need, personal development and general education goals affected freshmen's GPA and retention. Such findings reflect the value of adopting the non-cognitive variables for the development of new college admission standards.

The Non-Cognitive Model (NCM) proposed by Tracey and Sedlacek (1984) consists of eight psychosocial dimensions.

Positive Self-Concept. The successful individual expresses confidence in his or her ability to achieve the goal of graduating regardless of the obstacles that may arise. The individual expects to do well in both academic and non-academic arenas and makes positive statements about his or her self and assumes that he or she is able to handle any challenges that may come his or her way. There is a high level of self-efficacy and self-esteem.

Realistic Self-Appraisal System. The individual is able to recognize and accept background academic deficiencies and values working toward personal development. Students with a realistic self-appraisal system also appreciate and understand the rewards as well as the consequences of different levels of individual performance and develop an effective feedback interpretation system. They do not overreact or personalize criticism or rewards but see them as logical consequences of performance, even though evaluations can be biased.

Ability to Live in a Multicultural Society. Students able to live in a multicultural society have a realistic view of the multicultural society based on personal experience and understand the role of different socio-political systems impacting their lives and how these systems arbitrarily treat minority individuals. The individual has developed a sense of awareness of diverse cultures and accepts people from different racial cultural backgrounds. In addition, the person has made friends and worked with diverse people and can live with them in society in harmony.

Understanding and having the skills to live with the multicultural and imperfect society in the U.S. and elsewhere is important. Such individuals can "get things done" by getting around the socio-political systems, including any bias or discriminative policies or such practices from individual administrative units/personnel. They are not necessarily dissidents; instead they can get along well with the majority group in order to achieve their personal or minority group goals.

A Preference for Long-Term Goals. These individuals can set goals and work towards them for a significant amount of time without reinforcement. They are able to exhibit patience and experience partial fulfillment of a longer-term goal in small steps. These individuals have a future and a past orientation allowing them to look past the immediate situation and has insight into the benefits of planning for academic and non-academic goals.

Availability of a Strong Support Person. These individuals are able to recognize when they need help and are willing to ask for it. They may have had one or more specifically identified individuals such as a mentor who provided support and encouragement on a regular basis. They also recognize the difficulties inherent in being a "loner" and rarely rely solely on their own resources to address problems.

Successful Leadership Experiences. These individuals have had experience in leadership positions and have experience influencing and assisting others in both academic and non-academic situations. They are comfortable providing directions and advice to others and have experience mediating in disputes and disagreements between peers. Similarly, they have no problem taking appropriate action when a situation calls for it.

Demonstrated Community Service. These individuals identify with a social, cultural and/or racial group that has had a specific and long-term relationship within the community. Similarly, they have a history of involvement in community-based activities and/or organizations that have accomplished specific goals in the community setting.

Knowledge Acquired in a Field. These individuals have a non-traditional and possible culturally and/or racially based interest and experience based knowledge regarding a field or area that has not been formally studied in school. They have also developed innovative and creative ways in which to acquire information about a particular area.

The Non-Cognitive Questionnaire

The NCQ consists of measures of eight scales with possible score ranges printed in brackets in the following: (a) Positive Self-concept [7-27], (b) Realistic Self-Appraisal System[4-14], (c) Demonstrated Community Service [2-8], (d) Knowledge Acquired in a Field [2-8], (e) Successful Leadership Experience [3-13], (f) Preference of Long-Range Goals over Short-Term, Immediate Goals [3-13], (g) Ability to Understand and Cope with Racism [5-25], and (h) Availability of a Strong Support Person [3-15] (For details see Appendix One). Tracey and Sedlacek (1984) reported a 2-week test-retest reliability of a range from .74 to .94, with a median of .85 for the NCQ items. Interrater reliability on the three open-ended NCQ items ranged from .73 to 1.00. The scales also appear to have adequate construct validity; all eight constructs were correlated to questionnaire items (ranging from r = .31 to r = .71), except for the academic familiarity factor which appeared to be unrelated to the positive self-concept scale (Tracy and Sedlacek, 1987).

The Non-Cognitive Questionnaire (NCQ), which consists of 8 scales, has been adopted for college admissions, scholarships, academic programs, and student services at a handful of universities.

Many universities in the U.S.A. adopt an admission index for college admissions, and such admission indexes usually comprise standardized test scores such as Scholastic Aptitude Test (SAT) or American College Test (ACT) scores, and high school grade-point-average (GPA) or class rank. However, the SAT was not developed to be used as a primary admissions tool, but rather for comparison and measurement of the mathematical and verbal skills of a homogenous population with the desire to predict performance within the first year of college (The College Board, 1988, 1996). SAT scores were found to predict first-year academic performance, not beyond the first year (Ancis & Sedlacek, 1997; Baron & Norman, 1992; The College Board, 1988, 1996). Also, they more effectively predicted the college performance of Caucasians than that of ethnic minorities (Ting & Robinson, 1998; Tracey & Sedlacek, 1984, 1985, 1987; White & Sedlacek, 1986). Besides, SAT scores related more to the academic performance of regularly admitted students than specially admitted students who did not meet the admission criteria for admittance (White & Sedlacek, 1986). These standardized test scores were ineffective explaining, it would seem, some student attrition (Baron & Norman, 1992; Sowa, Thompson & Benett, 1989; Ting 2000a).

Noncognitive variables, on the other hand, produced variances (R^2 ranges from 20% to 35%) similar to or better than standardized test scores, estimating grades for different student groups as well. Noncognitive models showed mildly to moderately strong relationship to first-year student retention: Whites and Blacks (Hood, 1992; Tracey & Sedlacek, 1984, 1985, 1987), Asian Americans (Fuertes, Sedlacek, Liu, 1994; Ting, 2000b), Hispanics (Fuertes & Sedlacek, 1995), Mexican Americans (Aronba & Novy, 1990), specially-admitted students (Ting, 1997b; White & Sedlacek, 1986), low-income students (Ting, 1998), student athletes (Sedlacek & Adams-Gaston, 1992; Ting, 2000c), and international students (Boyer & Sedlacek, 1988). In addition, correlations with college grades and retention were significantly higher when the noncognitive variables were used in conjunction with standardized test scores and earlier grades.

After adopting the NCQ as part of their admissions package, the admissions committee at the Louisiana State University Medical School found that minority student enrollment has doubled to 21% with an 87% retention rate (Sedlacek, 1998). At North Carolina State University, longitudinal studies between 1996-2000 for 2600 students entering NC State in 1996 revealed that the variances explained by non-cognitive variables for specific student populations' GPAs were much higher than SAT scores (a range of 7 to 18%), such as female students (23%), Caucasian female students (25%), and African American males (29%) (Ting & Robinson, 1998). Also, the prediction models by college are stronger than the general models by whole university, 21.6% to 31.8% for college models vs. 16.7% to 24.7% for whole university, for example, agriculture and life sciences (n = 793) 31.8% and engineering (n = 735) 27.7%. This implies that college-specific profiles merit further attention and consideration for adoption. Different non-cognitive variables were related to students' performance in the four years of study. For example, positive self-concept and appraisal system are consistent variables throughout four years. However, preference for long-term goals, ability to cope with racism, and knowledge acquired in a field appear to be variables related to performance in latter years (Sedlacek, 1998; 2003). Sedlacek (2004) suggested that different institutions and different student groups, maybe different colleges within a university as well, interact in a wide variety of ways. It may be that, to be academically successfully in different colleges, students need a variety of academic skills and individual development. Since 2000, the Gates' Millennium Scholarship for Minority College Students has adopted the NCQ as its selection criterion.

The NCQ has also been adopted effectively as an intervention strategy within academic programs and student services in universities. For example, Sedlacek (1991) first reported an effective use of individual scores of the NCQ as assessing instrument and guidelines for individual counseling. Focused on the weak areas in the students' NCQ profile, they received individual counseling, tutorial, and other academic support services. In the results, the students were found improved their grades, retention, and graduation rate. Applying the non-cognitive variables as intervening strategies, the Excellent-Commitment-Effective-Learning (ExCEL) group, a small group intervention model was found to be useful for enhancing students' academic and psychosocial adjustment during the first year of university study (Ting, 1997b; Ting, 1999; Ting, Grant, & Plenert, 2000). A key for success appears to be learning in a small group and a focus on strengthening students' academic and psychosocial skills. Fogleman and Saeger (1985) reported adopting the NCQ as strategies for a successful application in a summer enrichment program for students in health majors. The students were found to have better academic adjustment and performance. Wawrzynski and Sedlacek (2003) discussed using the NCQ as an assessment instrument for nontraditional students to find out their weaknesses (lower scores on NCQ subscales) and needs in order to provide appropriate academic and student support services. Successes of the above groups and programs have strong implications for using the non-cognitive variables as strategies for student learning and development.

Chapter 2: Non-Traditional Students, First-Year Programs, and Services

Students from diverse backgrounds have substantially increased in population on college campuses since the 1970s. Gradually, the term "non-traditional students" has evolved to describe this very large part of college student populations, and is used usually in contrast to the "traditional students", i.e. White, middle-class, heterosexual males of European descent. From my perspective, non-traditional students are broadly defined as those who have a variety of backgrounds and a different set of experiences. These include older students, women, students of different sexual orientation, students of color, students from low-income families, and first-generation college students. More narrowly, non-traditional students can be defined as those with less power to control their lives and those who experience discrimination in the United States (Sedlacek, 2004). Sedlacek (2004) suggested using the Situational Attitude Scale (Sedlacek, 2004) and the Non-Cognitive Questions (Sedlacek, 2004) to determine if students are non-traditional. Such assessments can help determine if a group experiences prejudice and demonstrates abilities in way that differs from those with traditional experiences.

Because of their background and experiences, non-traditional students face some unique challenges. Some of them may not have the finances to attend or continue to study in college. Others may face racial discrimination and drop out; still others may be discriminated against because they are women. Yet a good proportion of them, about 25 to 30%, are first-generation college attendees and may have no role models or mentors to ask for help when they need support—another obstacle to add to their list of challenges.

Numerous first-year programs have been developed in the past two decades. The range of approaches and focuses varies from first-year seminars to adventure camps. However, a common goal can be found in these programs: enhancing student development and improving their academic performance and retention. Earlier pioneers in this area, like Noel's research group, have focused on first-year seminar classes as well as research studies on factors affecting student retention (Beal & Noel, 1979). John Gardener and his associates have developed the First-Year Seminar, and this model has influenced many first-year programs and services in our country. However, among all these programs, serving non-traditional students may not be emphasized.

Because first-year programs are designed to serve different institutions with different missions, first-year programs fall into several categories. In the first place, first-year programs can be divided into two types: mandated and voluntary participation. Mandated programs/services are designed to improve the academic quality of first-year college education. Many of these programs were developed as a response to the call for the need to improve undergraduate education since the 1990s. Students and parents were frustrated by the emphasis on research and graduate education in many universities. As a result, undergraduate education was neglected, causing problems such as large classes, instruction by teaching assistants, and poor faculty advising. In general, roughly one-third of the undergraduate classes in many research universities are taught by teaching assistants.

In response to the call, universities have established different mandated first-year programs. The most popular of these is a first-year seminar/class sequence such as "University 101". Students are required to attend one to two hours of classes every week on study skills, personal management, exploring career interests, and finding a major. Some classes include psychosocial development and cultural programs for promoting multiculturalism. Class size is usually a range from 15 to 20 students, and instructors may be professors or student affairs professionals. Some classes require one-on-one academic advising or counseling between the instructor and the student, while others may incorporate service learning activities. Even within this category of first-year programs, any school's requirements may "look very different from another's."

First-year programs can also be grouped into curricular and co-curricular programs/classes. The National Survey of First-Year Practices in 2000, conducted by the Policy Center on the First Year of College, can provide useful information because it was a random sample of 621 institutions in U.S. stratified by Carnegie classifications. According to the survey, curricular practices include first-year seminars, learning communities, first-year classes in residence halls, service learning, supplemental instruction, early alert systems, and distance education and on-line first year courses. Co-curricular practices include student orientation, leadership programs, student government, programs in residence halls, and Greek life.

The survey found that who teaches first-year classes and the size of first-year classes depend on academic discipline, institutional size, and institutional type. For example, across all institutional sizes and types, first-year English tends to be taught in a section size of no more than twenty-five students (89%). Also, the survey reveals that first-year seminars are offered by 80% of four-year and 62% of two-year institutions in U.S. These seminars aim to help students adjust into the academic and social life and assist in their transition to college. By definition, a seminar is a small discussion-based on a course in which students and their instructors exchange ideas and information, and the rationale for first-year seminars are the adjustment needs of students (Hunter & Linder, 2005, p. 275). Successful seminars are the ones offering academic credit, centered in the first-year curriculum, collaborating between faculty and student affairs professionals, providing instructor training and development, compensating/rewarding instructors for teaching the seminar, involving upper-level students, and being periodically assessed for their effectiveness (Barefoot & Fidler, 1996).

First-year seminar is not new; it was preceded by the formation of a system of faculty advisers at John Hopkins University in 1877, and later a board of freshmen advisors at Harvard University in 1889 (Gordon, 1989). In the past twenty years, first-year seminars have proliferated in higher education campuses. Among all of these programs, the National Resources Center for the First-Year Experience and Students in Transition has a leading role in promoting first-year seminars through research, programs and services; they contribute to development and discourse by sponsoring conferences, conducting research and disseminating new information.

Types of First-Year Programs

Types of first-year seminars include extended orientation seminars (the most common type) (Hunter & Linder, 2005), academic seminars, and others. Sixty-two percent of institutions in the national survey who offer first-year seminars offer an extended orientation type, which focuses are on student survival and success techniques. Extended orientations are taught by faculty or student affairs professionals, and may also be credited as part of the institution's requirements. Appalachian State University, for example, offers a three-credit seminar that focuses on building community and introducing institutional information. The class also includes outdoor activities, such as a low-ropes challenge experience, for team building development.

The second most common type of first-year seminar are academic seminars with uniform curriculum across sections (17% in the national survey) or those with topics varying from section to section (13% in the survey) (Hunter & Linder, 2005). The seminar is either required or taken as an elective; it can be a part of general education. It focuses on an academic theme common to all sections and other skills such as learning and studying, critical thinking, and writing. For example, at North Carolina State University, students at First-Year College are required to take a 1 credit course on class information, selecting a major/career, developing study and learning skills and providing community service. Academic seminars on various topics are organized based on faculty members' individual areas of academic or personal interest and expertise. The University of Michigan also offers such seminars, taught by faculty from various disciplines that focus on topics like *The Poetry of Everyday Life, Inventing Race,* and *Traditional China through Its Most Famous Novel: The Story of the Stone.*

Other types of seminars include professional, discipline-linked, and basic study skills seminars, which combine to make a total of about 9% of all first-year seminars in the national survey. Professional and discipline-linked seminars focus on preparing students to enter a discipline/profession such as engineering, medicine or law. Basic study skills seminars are offered to students who are not academically ready for universities, such as high-risk students and students with low admission scores. They emphasize attending class, reading, note-taking, revision, and preparing for tests. On some campuses, first-year-seminars combine elements from some of all of the above seminar types, such as Wellesley College's writing seminars that relate to the instructor's academic interest and expertise as well as incorporating a focus on thinking skills.

Innovative or "especially successful" instructional activities on the 2000 National Survey of First-Year Seminar Programming (National Resource Center, 2002), include the use of high technology for communication (e.g. emails and internet), written assignments, and exploration activities into careers and academic majors. Other successful cases were an etiquette banquet at Georgetown

College, the construction of a diversity quilt at Moorpark College, and a simulation of natural selection at Columbia College (Hunter & Linder, 2005).

One of the trends in first-year seminar curricula is to link seminars to learning communities, service-learning and community service, partnerships with student affairs professionals, and residence life. Other trends include shifting focus to include discipline-specific content, offering letter-graded seminars, more gains for students in more than one contact hour per week, a slight increase of upper-level undergraduate students as teaching assistants or mentors, sections for special populations such as academically under-prepared students, honors students, and students in a learning community. More institutional support, more focus on helping students assimilate to and engage in college-level learning, and academic skills are the most frequently reported goals.

Case Studies

The following case studies describe a few examples of the first-year programs in our country, including the popular first-year program at the University of South Carolina.

University 101 – at the University of South Carolina

University 101 at the University of South Carolina was first introduced in 1972 for freshmen. Now, it is a three-credit hour, letter-graded course. The course aims to help first-year students adjust to the university, develop a better understanding of the learning process, and acquire essential academic success skills. It provides an orientation to the functions and resources of the university and also offers a support group for students transitioning to college by examining problems common to the first-year experience. Approximately 80% of the incoming freshman class enrolls in the course. A majority of the students take the general sections; while some colleges and programs require their students to take specialized sections of the course. University 101 is offered in every semester, although most of the students enroll in the fall. The course is taught in small groups (20-25 students) by faculty members and student development professionals. Undergraduate peer leaders and/or graduate leaders assist in some sections.

In addition to classroom activities, the students are required to attend four presentations: alcohol and drugs, career development, sexual assault and relationship violence, and library information and resources. In order to provide such presentations to the students, University 101 collaborates with GAMMA Peer Educators on the alcohol and drug use, career center on career development, the Office for Sexual Health and Violence Prevention on sexual assault and violence prevention, and library on the library/information literacy presentation. According to institutional research, University 101 students have been found to modify their sexual behaviors, reduce health risks, and make more responsible decisions as a result of this course component. After launching their program over 30 years ago, the University 101 department has created four courses to help students become successful academically. University 101, a first-year student seminar, may be the first one in America and is the longest running course among the four courses at the University of South Carolina. University 201 focuses on how to conduct research; residence students are engaged in seminar-like class discussions in University 290. Finally, seniors who are in transition to their career or graduate school enroll in University 401 to reflect on their college experience. Skills are the most frequently reported goals.

First Year College at North Carolina State University

The First Year College (FYC) at NC State encourages first year students to "chart their courses" toward becoming involved, committed, and successful members of the university. FYC is designed for students who prefer a year of general study accompanied with major and career guidance. FYC also provides opportunities for students to enhance their academic and social integration into the new community. FYC advisors play a key role in the student experience by providing individual academic advising and counseling to students. In addition, they facilitate and teach a first year orientation course, USC 101/103, for their FYC students each fall and spring.

There are four goals in the USC 101 mission:
    (a) To provide a smooth transition from high school to college,
    (b) To develop strategies to achieve academic and personal success,
    (c) To promote self discovery and awareness of others, and
    (d) To explore majors and careers.

In addition to classroom experience, FYC also requires students to attend educational, vocational, social, cultural, and wellness forums/events. The Super Forum Events are organized by the FYC around events that are significant to the university or the larger community outside of the university. Students also can be selected to serve on the FYC Student Council and receive points as credits to their USC 101/102. Finally, by the end of the spring semester, the students are asked to gather their work in USC 101/102 by compiling a portfolio, which reflects their learning through the course, and reflect on their majors/careers.

Another feature of the FYC is the FYC Village, which is a learning community designed to enhance the college transition and learning experiences of the first-year residents by providing a safe and welcoming environment for them to meet peers from diverse backgrounds and cultures, develop a sense of community, and connect to the larger University community. FYC students may choose to live anywhere, however, two residence halls are exclusively reserved for them. At their residence halls, FYC students can take their USC 101/102 classes and many general education required classes, receive academic advising, and have peer support from a Resident Assistant and Resident Mentor.

The third and final category of approach to the first-year program/service is organizing groups or workshops for students who will voluntarily participate. Usually, these groups do not carry any academic credits or units and are led by counselors or professional advisors. Many of these groups are co-sponsored by a few student services offices such as advising centers and multicultural student services, or counseling centers and women's centers or residential services. The objectives of the program are, like those of their mandatory and curricular counterparts, enhancing adjustment and improving study skills. Voluntary programs developed from orientation (Mullendore & Banahan, 2005) with focuses for special populations such as students of color, disadvantaged students, adult students, and international students. They may be extended orientation programs, first-year workshops, developmental programs, study skills seminars, and intentional workshops such as on diversity issues. All of them seem to contribute to college satisfaction and increased retention (Mullendore & Banahan, 2005). The Excellent Commitment and Effective Learning (ExCEL) program is a good example of such group intervention.

Chapter 3: The ExCEL Group—Developmental Structured Groups, Theories, and Strategies

The first year in college is a time of adjustment and turmoil (Chickering & Reisser, 1993; Erikson, 1997). Because problems encountered in the adjustment process can cause students to drop out (Gerald, 1992), students' adjustment and academic performance during their freshman year in universities have become important topics in research and professional practice in higher education. A number of theoretical models have been developed to describe various factors affecting college student adjustment and academic performance (Astin, 1997; Pascarella & Terenzini, 2005; Tinto, 1993). Over twenty years, Sedlacek and his colleagues (2004) studied a set of non-cognitive variables and developed the Non-Cognitive Questionnaire (NCQ), a pre-enrollment instrument. The NCQ explores psychological, cultural, and social factors in explaining academic success and retention of college students. Through their research, Tracey and Sedlacek (1989) identified eight non-cognitive factors proved to be related to academic success: positive self-concept, realistic self-appraisal, ability to cope with racism, a preference of long term goals, a strong support person, leadership experience, demonstrated community service, and acquired knowledge in a field.

The Excellent Commitment and Effective Learning (ExCEL) group proposed here is based on the non-cognitive variables model; it uses a developmental structured-group approach (Corey & Corey, 2003; Gazda, 1989; Rose, 1985). The group's purpose is to improve participating students' (note 1). study skills, psychosocial adjustment and academic achievement and is an example of the third category of program defined in the proceeding chapter: a voluntary first-year program based on noncognitive variables.

Case Study

A non-cognitive variables model has potential to produce recognizable changes in individuals' skill and confidence levels. Consider the following real case (name changed), illustrating the adjustment issues from a non-cognitive assessment. Non-cognitive problems are identified and discussed in the case.

Case Study
Mee Who

Mee Who is an Asian American woman who is 24 years old, about 5 feet 2 inches tall and weighs around 120 to 130 pounds. She is a low-income first generation college student. She is a sophomore and her major is social work. Her family immigrated to the U.S. from Laos seven years ago. Her home is only 40 miles away, she always goes home during weekends.

She has two older brothers and two younger sisters. Mee needs to take care of her sisters when she is at home because her mother has a chronic illness and stays in a hospital. Mee has received federal and state grants and loans for her education. She also works about 8 to 10 hours per week on campus. Mee feels challenged in her language skills and studies; she also has low self-confidence. On campus, she is Secretary for the Asian American Student Association.

In her studies, Mee cannot summarize her reading or notes well. She does not study regularly; instead she tends to cram before tests or examinations. When Mee attends classes, she still has problems taking notes and following instructions. She says that her instructors speak too fast. Therefore, she is always confused in her classes. As a minority student, she has also gone to the Multicultural Services Office for advising. Overall, she struggles to find balance among her studies, part-time work, social activities and commitments at home.

Counselor's Analysis

As Mee faces her language and studying problems, she also suffers from a low self-concept because of her appearance and immigrant status. It appears that she is confused in her classes and is not sure how to study well in her major. She has low self-appraisal ability. However, she is involved with Asian American students, which is a good social support for her. She is rather active on campus; meanwhile she has to work, study, take care of her sisters at home as well. She cannot divide her time well among her activities and other commitments.

During the exit interview, she identifies some changes in the following areas: (1) increased time for studying, (2) knew more how to evaluate performance and own self, (3) learned skills to summarize reading notes, and (4) can find solutions to problems. Yet, she still needs to improve her English through tutorials and continue to receive counseling.

The Excellent Commitment and Effective Learning (ExCEL) Group Model

The Excellent Commitment and Effective Learning (ExCEL) program is a structured counseling intervention group available through college student services. ExCEL is grounded in human/student development theory and based on the establishment of personal and caring relationship between the student and the advisor/counselor (Ender, Winston, and Miller, 1982). The ExCEL program is oriented to small groups and focuses on goals, empirical experiences, and coping-skill-training including cognitive-behavioral strategies.

The content and strategies of the ExCEL group are based on Sedlacek's (2004) non-cognitive model. Sedlacek (1991) reported using a strategy emphasizing non-cognitive variables when advising non-traditional students. He collected general personal information, identified psychosocial areas of concerns by using the Non-Cognitive Questionnaire (NCQ) (Tracey & Sedlaek, 1984), and employed that information as a guide for further advising activities. In his results, he found that both students' academic performance and campus social lives were enhanced. The non-cognitive model appears to be an efficacious theoretical approach for designing retention programs for students. Ting and Robinson (1998) asserted that non-cognitive variables effectively predicted academic performance and student retention for different student populations including: African-Americans, Asian-Americans, Hispanics, Caucasians, international students, and low-income and first-generation students.

In addition to noncognitive variables, study skills also appear to be an important factor affecting academic performance. Learning styles and study skills of students were good predictors of their grades and retention (Nisbet, Ruble, & Schurr, 1982; Olejnik & Nist, 1992; Watkins, 1986).

Small Group Orientation

The ExCEL operates like a small group orientation. According to Rose (1989), the small group orientation creates a sense of togetherness, frequency and varied opportunities for mutual reinforcement, allows members to learn to deal with the idiosyncrasies of other individuals, and allows for the use of group strategies. Yalom believes that small group orientation creates the sense of "universality" (Yalom & Leszcz, 2005) or, "we're all in the same boat." Duncan stated,

> I think Yalom has really captured the essence of what group work is all about and, in my opinion, universality is extremely effective in group work. Once group members understand this concept and internalize it, other concepts seem to fall into place pretty readily" (cited in Forester-Miller, 1993, p. 171).

Being in a group and hearing about others' struggles with their problems helps reduce guilty or helpless feelings, as listening to tales of successful recoveries from problems or coping with personal weaknesses may spark hopes and ideas for other members' personal changes. In small groups, members can help one another in the changing process through discussion, assessment, and working together. Yalom and Leszcz (2005) describe the phenomenon as "altruism." Clients change not only through receiving, but also from intrinsic acts of giving support, assurance, suggestions, and insight.

Yalom and Leszcz (2005) believe groups are a microcosm of the real world. A group member naturally plays out his or her life problems in small groups, and learns how to live well within the group before he or she can transfer this learning into the real world. In group process, group leaders may introduce effective group skills such as group exercises, multiple modeling, group feedback, group brainstorming, and mutual reinforcement (Rose, 1989).

In the ExCEL group, student members come from diverse backgrounds but face common challenges of adjusting to the first year of college life. The ExCEL group targets students from nontraditional backgrounds including low-income, first-generation, students of color, older and disabled students; many of them are academically under-prepared or at-risk. Studies show that loneliness may be the most common feeling among these students; when students get together in groups, they realize that they are not alone anymore.

Through the process of group activities, students develop a sense of community within the group. Plentiful opportunities exist in the group process for them to learn about successful experiences from one another and from the group leader. Therefore, they are encouraged to make changes. Meanwhile, the ExCEL group leader applies specific group strategies adopted from the findings of non-cognitive studies (Sedlacek, 1991; Ting, 1997a; Ting, 2000; Ting, 2001; Ting & Robinson, 1998; Tracey & Sedlacek, 1984; Tracey & Sedlacek, 1989). These strategies promote increased academic self-confidence, enhanced self-appraisal skills, establishing long-term goals, finding a support person, becoming involved in student activities, serving in a community, increasing knowledge in a field, and learning to live in a multicultural society—all of the factors that predict persistence in university programs.

In the group process, norms are always established to enable the group to work effectively. When the norms work well, they serve as powerful therapeutic tools. Such norms may include regular attendance, active participation, mutual respect, being open to criticism, and supporting one another. There may be times that the norms are broken or improper norms exist, such as frequent tardiness or refusal to participate in group activities; then the group leader work on restoring or maintaining the group norms (Corey & Corey, 2003; Yalom & Leszcz, 2005). Skills that group leaders must master include modification of norms, renegotiation, changing communication patterns, and group pressure.

Studies show that group therapy seems to be at least as effective and more efficient in terms of cost and outcomes as a one-on-one approach. ExCEL's choice of small groups for therapy and training is based on empirical studies in college counseling, student services, and group work. Specifically, the ExCEL group adopts the strategies derived from the non-cognitive model (Sedlacek, 2004) which have been empirically proven (Stonehouse & Ting, 2000; Ting, 1997b; Ting, 1999; Ting, Grant, & Plenert, 2000; Ting & Robinson, 1998).

Goal Orientation

The ExCEL group is goal-oriented, and the program assumes that the pursuit of academics in college is different from high school. For example, college students are expected to work more independently in their academics than they are in high schools. Also, it assumes that in a larger community and more diverse student population, college freshmen need to adjust to new living and social challenges. According to the Chronicle of Higher Education Almanac (2005), 44 % undergraduates are part-time students, and 38% are adult students. The challenge of adjusting to a university's academic expectations and integrating to the community, for the large number of commuting and part-time adult students, is huge.

Therefore, the common group goal for the ExCEL program is for new students to enhance their adjustment to college life. The ExCEL group attempts to offer interactive activities in the group and provide a comfortable and safe setting; ExCEL is a place for support and academic and psychosocial development. For example, at the end of the session on "Learning to Live in a Multicultural Society," all group members will actively participate in role plays on multicultural diversity relationships, will (hopefully) feel safe discussing controversial situations, and will have learned some multicultural skills.

In a small group, individual goals which complement or enrich the group goals are also emphasized. Consider a group member who wants to find a mentor through the group experience. Another may desire to search for a major and get to know more friends. Table 3.1 shows a list of appropriately related group and individual goals for a sample ExCEL group:

Group Goals	Individual Goals
1. Learn study skills.	1. Improve on math skills.
2. Improve test taking skills.	2. Reduce test anxiety.
3. Increase awareness on self-concept.	3. Be happier.
4. Refine self-appraisal skills.	4. Find a major.
5. Improve knowledge in a field.	5. Look for financial aid.
6. Develop personal long term goals.	6. Find a mentor.
7. Increase involvement in student activities.	7. Make more friends.
8. Serve more in a community.	8. Serve in my church fellowship
9. Develop multicultural skills.	9. Join student government.

Table 3.1: Examples of Group Goals and Individual Goals

Note that individual goals are always personal, specific, and unique. However, in most cases, these personal goals can be integrated into the common group goals. Usually, personal goals that are too different or distant from the common ExCEL goals are screened out. Through the informational meeting before the group is formed, these students learn about the common group goals. If potential group members do not agree with the group goals, they may not join the group, or they may have to adjust their personal goals.

Developmental Approach/Training Orientation

The ExCEL group adopts a developmental approach emphasis on training as a preferred mode of group treatment. This emphasis follows a tradition of counseling focused on development and training (Gazda, 1989; Gazda, Horne, & Ginter, 2001; Rose, 1989). Gazda (1989) proposed the following concepts for development:

    (1) The core of functioning or dysfunctioning is interpersonal. It is assumed that interpersonal processes reflect intrapersonal dynamics, or conversely what is going on within the individual is manifested in what goes on between individuals.

    (2) The core of the helping process (learning or relearning) is interpersonal. Positive interpersonal learning experiences can correct destructive interpersonal learning experiences.

(3) Group processes are the preferred mode of working with difficulties in interpersonal function.

Gazda argued that we can do anything in group treatment that we can do in individual treatment—and more. By nature, groups are interpersonal; they offer group members the means not only to relate to the group leader and oneself, with the leader's guidance, but also to relate to other group members and to the group as a whole. Group processes offer the prospect for the greatest amount of learning for the greatest number of people at one time (Gazda, 1989).

The primary nature of the ExCEL group is training—training for success at a university. Many group authors have discussed the benefits of using structured groups for therapy and training purposes (Corey & Corey, 2003; Gazda, 1989; Rose, 1989; Shaffer & Galinsky, 1989; Yalom & Leszcz, 2005). The purpose of the ExCEL group falls between training and therapy: according to Rose (1989), therapy is more intense, deals with more complex problems, includes more broad-based learning, while training provides group members with more information and opportunities to discuss and practice that information. In terms of goals, greater emphasis is placed on both group and individual goals in therapy than in training groups. In fact, the processes of training and therapy orientation fall on a continuum: a key factor to distinguish the two types is available time. Groups meeting up to 18 sessions tend to fall under therapy in the continuum, while groups meeting for 8 sessions, such as the ExCEL group, can be placed in the middle on the continuum (Rose, 1989). Group meetings fewer than 8 sessions will fall under training groups, such as groups at new student orientation or one-day workshops. However, the principles of teaching and learning in groups on the training-therapy continuum remain the same.

Perhaps the first program employing training directly as a preferred mode of group treatment involved training parents of emotionally disturbed children and comparing the results to those of traditional parental counseling (Carhuff & Bierman, cited in Rose, 1989). Carhuff and Bierman found that significant changes occurred in the relationship between parents and between the parents and their children in follow-up studies. Another study shows that support and training groups for 28 women improved their ability to deal with shame, secrecy, and the stigmatization associated with incest (Herman & Schatzow, 1984). Also, men reported that a training group helped them manage their anger, develop more male friends, become more assertive and happier, and feel more content with themselves after 16 weekly group sessions (Corey & Corey, 2003).

However, limitations of the training approach sometimes relate to the rigid employment of the programs (Rose, 1989). If the group leader is not shaped by feedback from the group members, and if s/he does not modify the group treatment procedures accordingly, the program can be harmful or useless. These situations can be handled by the group leader's increased awareness, a co-leadership model, and different types of individual treatment that are offered concurrently with the group experience such as one-on-one advising outside of the group.

Cognitive Behavioral Strategies

To achieve the group and individual goals, the ExCEL group adopts cognitive and behavioral skills for group intervention. Cognitive skills focus on intervention with group members' thinking, cognitive images, attitudes, values, and beliefs and include guided imagery, modeling, and reframing (Cormier & Nurius, 2003). Behavioral skills intervention works on clients' actions, such as role playing, meditation, relaxation, systematic desensitization, self-statements, self management, and self monitoring.

Guided Imagery is usually used to change feelings and emotions related to anxiety, migraine, physical problems, allergy, and grieving. In guided imagery, a person focuses on positive thoughts or images while imagining a discomforting or anxiety-arousing activity or situation (Corimer & Nurius, 2003). By focusing on positive and pleasant images, the person is able to "block" the painful, fearful, or anxiety–provoking situation. In the ExCEL group, guided imagery is used during the session on positive self-confidence to help the students understand their self images. In the process, group members focus on examining and enhancing their self confidence in an image fantasy of their self as a blooming flower. This exercise helps the students become more self-confident (see the following table for detailed procedures).

EXCEL GROUP
SESSION
UNDERSTANDING SELF-CONCEPT

Objectives;
1. Student will understand more about who they are.
2. Student will identify their personal strengths and weakness.
3. Students will become more aware about who they are.

Procedures:
I. Reviewing last meeting – 10 minutes
II. Guided Imagery: the rose Journey – 20 minutes

Objectives: to allow students to use their imaginations in order to reflect upon their self-images.
Procedures;
1. Relaxation: The students' relax their upper bodies from hands and arms to shoulder, neck, and head; then their lower bodies from waist down to legs, feet, and ankles.
2. Now, imagine you are a flower (the rose journey), describe the flower (you):
  - what is the type of the flower?
  -describe how it stands: its height, color, and features.
  -describe the surrounds: Any other plants near you? How do they grow?
  -describe the background: Where is the flower located? Describe it.

> 3. Now imagine you are walking alone on a beach which is quiet and empty:
>   - The breeze is blowing on your face. Feel the breeze; How do you feel?
>   - You find a jar in the sand. You kneel down and pick it up. The jar is empty.
>   - Now write 3 things about your current anxieties/worries on a piece of paper.
>   - What are the three things?
>   - Put the piece of paper in the jar.
>   - Use your whole strength to throw the jar into the sea.
>   - You can see the jar drifting off and becomes smaller until it disappears.
>   - The piece of paper is gone now. How do you feel now?
> 4. In your own time, you may open your eyes.
> 5. Process the rose "journey" in your group; focus on the relationship between the self and the flower.
>
> III. A Review about You - 60 minutes
>   Discuss with students about how they evaluate their own "self." Examples of topics for discussion: personal strengths and weaknesses, self image, ethnic/racial identity development.
>
> IV. Assignments: complete the table about self-concept.

Modeling can be broken into observational and participant types. Observational modeling uses films, videotapes, role models, desired thoughts or self-talk to enable the clients to imitate. Participant modeling is used to demonstrate desired behaviors in vivo, and the client is guided through performance of the behavioral consequence. In the group session on living in a multicultural society, assertive responses are taught through the group leader's in vivo demonstration. Role models of racial and ethnic minorities and women are discussed.

Reframing helps clients to access and determine the relations among their perceptions, cognitions, emotions and actions; to identify how clients interpret their situations and experiences; and to urge them to substitute a new interpretive frame (Gendlin in Cormier & Nurius, 2003, p. 395). Reframing is used in many ExCEL group sessions, for example, during the session on developing a realistic self-appraisal system, clients are challenged through conversation, reflection on a form, and group interaction to identify, understand, and reframe the perspectives on their academic situations. In practice, the group leader will use a series of open-ended questions to help the students explore their self-appraisal system: "Are you aware of the evaluation/grading methods of your classes? Can you share two examples?" "How do you evaluate your performance in classes?" "What are the guidelines or criteria you use? Give an example." Gradually, the group leader will move in deeper and help the client to reframe their perceptions and self-evaluation. More guiding questions are asked, such as "Share about a class in which you are not doing well, comparatively.

How do you explain the reasons for this?" These types of questions will challenge the student to begin to think from alternative perspectives about their self-evaluation system. Other questions may be used, e.g., "How do you study for this class?" Finally, when the student begins to change his or her perspectives, more open-ended questions are used to help him or her explore from a reframed perspective with general questions first, such as "How might you improve your performance?" Then, more specific questions are asked to help the student develop a new perspective, including, "What are the resources or help you can get on campus or from your family, friends, etc for your studying?" and "How do you respond to advice or feedback from a friend or your major advisor?" At the end of the meeting, in order to help the student consolidate their learning, the group leader invites the group to summarize what they learned from the meeting.

Role Playing is defined as the practice of roles in simulated conditions (Rose, 1989). Role playing is always designed for group members to make changes, broaden participation, and increase group cohesion. In the EXCEL group, role playing is used to teach specific skills such as assertiveness, self understanding, and communication. For example, in the session on multicultural skills, in the beginning, the group leader sets up some rules to ensure a non-judgmental and safe environment for this exercise. Then, when the group leader calls out names of ethnic groups, genders, religions, and the like, group members immediately say the uncensored thoughts associated with the names. Next, the group leader asks for feedback from the group. In the next exercise in the same session, students form groups in twos that belong to the same ethnic, gender or religious group. The first person points finger to the partner and says the negative stereotypes associated with the group; the second person listens. The partners then switch roles and exchange feedback. Next, the first person says things they are proud of concerning their group, and partners exchange feedback. Finally, the group leader processes these activities with the whole group.

Relaxation asks clients to relax by becoming aware of the sensations of tensing and relaxing their bodies. In practice, with the client focused on breathing, the group leader instructs him or her to tense and relax his or her body from head to feet or feet to head. Relaxation is always used as a warm-up activity to prepare the client for imagery exercises or systematic desensitization.

Systematic Desensitization is a popular skill for coping with phobias, anxiety related to public speaking, mathematics, test-taking, and dietary restraint (Cormier & Nurius, 2003). The concept is founded on the classical theory of behavioral conditioning that we can relearn (through counter-conditioning) new behaviors and change bad behaviors learned from our environment (conditioned). We can change our own conditioning, therefore, through systematic desensitization and counter-conditioning process. In the ExCEL group, this skill is usually applied in individual counseling meetings between the group leader and the student. The therapist identifies emotion-provoking situations and asks the client to put them in a hierarchy. Then, the client receives training of counterconditioning responses, to be followed by imagery assessment checking the relearning progress and developing scene presentations for different situations.

Self-Management Strategies include self-statements, self monitoring, stimulus control, self-reward and self-efficacy (Cormier & Nurius, 2003). Self management processes operate through four principal subfunctions: (1) self-monitoring of one's behavior, its components, and its effects; (2) judgment of one's behavior; (3) affective self-reactions; and (4) self-efficacy. Self-monitoring refers to observing and recording the client's own particular behavior (thoughts, feelings and actions) and interactions with environmental events. Stimulus control consists of prearranging antecedents or cues to increase or decrease the client's performance of a target behavior. Self-reward is giving clients themselves a positive stimulus following a desired response. For example, in a group session on time management, self-monitoring is applied to students when they are asked to record their activities in a weekly log and to share their experience with the group. Then, they are asked to insert stimulus between major blocks of study/work time and to self-reward for successfully following a new daily activity schedule. Through this activity, students learn to reflect upon their current time management and to learn new skills with which to make better use of their time.

Extra Group Interventions

Yalom & Leszcz (2005) points to extra group intervention strategies as being as important as those that occur within the group. Many authors discuss the benefits of reinforcing activities for better results (Corey & Corey, 2003; Donigian & Malnati, 1997; Gazda, 1989). These strategies involve the group members in self-reflecting on personal development, self-observing their changes, discussing with their families, trying out new behaviors, and self-evaluating their progress. For example, after discussing a strong support person for students, the group members are asked to look for such a person, and to report their activities with the support person during the remaining group sessions. Parallel with group sessions, often the ExCEL group also includes individual counseling. Group leaders meet with the group members individually a few times during the group process. Such individual meetings allow individual attention and further exploration into a person's developmental issues and training for improvements/changes. Usually, the group leader focuses on the weaknesses of the student based on the non-cognitive assessment.

Ethical Issues in the ExCEL Group

Ethical issues are important in group work, and they are carefully considered in the ExCEL group. A professional disclosure statement describing confidentiality, theoretical orientation, nature, purpose(s) and goals of the group, group benefits, structure of the group, and roles and responsibilities of group members and leaders is included in the recruiting material. The qualifications of the group leader are also addressed. Such information conforms to the *Best Practice Guidelines in Group Work* (Association for Specialists in Group Work, 2005).

For the purposes of maintaining ethical integrity, prospective group members receive a fact sheet about the ExCEL group. They learn that they are expected to attend all group meetings and participate in the group activities and in the evaluation process. Also, students are provided a consent form describing the purpose for the group, voluntary participation and withdrawal without penalty, and the source of funding. They are asked to sign the form and consent to participate in the group and a related study and to a review of their academic records.

Preparing the group is important to successful group outcomes (Association for Specialists in Group Work, 2005). In addition to legal considerations, screening for prospective group members is key. In practice, at the information meeting, students are provided with group information including objectives, an outline and topics for each session, roles of the group leader and members, and methods of evaluation. Questions from prospective members are answered. At the end of the meeting, students may sign up for the group or they may register later. Students will provide their personal information in the registration form, will answer a few questions about their concerns and will provide a brief mental health history. Then the group leader will review the information for screening. Since the ExCEL group is not a therapy group, only students who do not have current mental health problems under DSM-IV TR such as depression, delusion, etc are included in the ExCEL group. If students are found to have mental health problems, they are referred to the counseling center on campus for individual therapy.

Confidentiality is more difficult to maintain in groups than during individual therapy, although breaches of confidentiality are rare in my professional experience. Also, expectations for keeping confidentiality can be communicated in the group forming process and consequences of such breaches can be discussed in the beginning sessions. This is why leading small groups such as ExCEL requires professional counseling and small group training, which helps reduce possible problems.

Group practitioners may also take measures to avoid possible problems or risks for small groups. However, I also recognize the limitations of groups; not every client and problem can be treated solely through groups. The ExCEL group is usually easier to organize with administrative support, and in related studies, most of the ExCEL group members are recruited through an admissions process (including specially admitted students) or the students are required to attend such groups because of their low academic status, such as enrollment in remedial courses for the academically at-risk. Challenges for the ExCEL group include mutual trust and confidentiality issues. It takes time for a group to develop mutual trust, particularly with eight to ten sessions, but if mutual trust is not established early, it may affect group cohesiveness and outcomes.

Evaluation

Evaluation for the ExCEL group covers study skills, academic achievement and student retention. To examine the changes in students' study skills, the Learning and Study Strategies Inventory (LASSI; Weinstein & Palmer, 1987) was adopted. The LASSI is designed to measure students' use of learning strategies and study methods and consists of 10 scales: Attitude, Motivation, Time Management, Coping with Anxiety, Concentration, Information Processing, Selecting Main Ideas, Study Aids, Self Testing, and Test Skills. A pre-and-post test method was adopted comparing students' LASSI scores in ExCEL groups. Significant improvements were found on the subscales of Concentration, Information Processing, Selecting Main Ideas, Coping with Anxiety and Self-Testing Skills among students in ExCEL group outcomes (Ting, 1997b; Ting, 1999; Ting, Grant, & Plenert, 2000).

In addition to the LASSI, GPA was used as an indicator of academic performance, and student registration status represented student retention. Significant differences were found in the semester mean GPA of the treatment and control groups. Treatment group mean GPAs were better than those of the control group (Stonehouse and Ting, 2000; Ting, 1997b; Ting, 1999; Ting, Grant, & Plenert, 2000). Student retention was defined as student registration status (enrolling = 1; dropping out = 0). The mean retention rate for ExCEL groups after the first year was higher than that of the control group.

Finally, the Non-Cognitive Questionnaire (NCQ) was used as a baseline for noncognitive facets of development. In the beginning of the group sessions, the ExCEL students completed the NCQ. At the end of the program, the authors also interviewed the students individually to find out their perceptions of psychosocial changes based on their profiles from the preliminary NCQ. Noncognitive student development always helps explain overall changes in academic performance and study skills.

To sum up, the ExCEL group is goal and training-oriented and well structured based on a developmental framework. The rationales, orientation and ethical issues for the group are discussed in this chapter. This chapter focuses on an introduction to the ExCEL group theory and concepts and covers its assumptions and definitions, and empirical evidence. In later chapters, the author will discuss the procedures, group process and dynamics, group skills, and detailed reports of some ExCEL programs. The chapter on group process contains detailed content about the ExCEL group sessions which the reader may find it useful to peruse before continuing.

Notes

1. In this chapter, I tend to use group leader or therapist to name the person who leads the group process. I use students, group members, and clients interchangeably to name the group participants.

Chapter 4:
Establishing the ExCEL Group

The Excellent Commitment and Effective Learning (ExCEL) Group is founded on the structured group model. The ExCEL group is particularly designed for non-traditional students including women, students of color, older students, low-income, and first-generation students. To establish the ExCEL group, a group leader should first identify the target student population and ask a series of questions to determine the students' needs. Is the university facing student retention challenges? How do non-traditional students perform compared to traditional students? If the non-traditional students are trailing behind, what are the reasons? Also, the group leader should find out what types of services are offered to non-traditional students on campus. Are these programs effective improving student performance and development? After studying the need for intervention and specifying the target student group, the group leader may start to plan the ExCEL group.

In the planning phase, I encourage collaboration, which helps student recruitment: maybe two or three student services/academic offices working together. Collaboration increases student's attention and interests, thus enhances student participation. Also, collaboration incorporates the perspectives and expertise of different professionals from different disciplines, and finally, it may avoid duplications and saves resources.

The purpose of the ExCEL group is to help first-year students improve their academic performance and retention rates by teaching studying skills and psychosocial development topics through related educational, advising and group activities. The ExCEL group design is based on the aforementioned empirical research in ability assessment and college admissions, which has demonstrated that both cognitive and non-cognitive factors affect students' academic performance and retention rate. This proposed group facilitates first-year students' study skill development and promotes their psychological, social and cultural development. Repeated research studies show that ExCEL program enhances students' GPA and retention.

The ExCEL group adopts a structured, thematic-centered group model with a group size of about 10 to 12 students. Group members are usually first-year students, particularly with a non-traditional background. Each group meets for 8 to 10 weekly sessions which are about 90 minutes each in length. At each meeting, members will interact and discuss on a topic. The group leader will start by introducing the topic briefly, then the leader will facilitate group members to share personally about the topic and interact in role-plays and activities. Throughout the process, members will learn from the leader and one another. Sometimes, home assignments reinforcing the discussed topics will be distributed at the end of the meeting, and individual meetings are also a part of the program; students will see the group leader for additional support and help. The group starts to meet in the beginning of a semester, typically in the fall semester, and ends around mid-term. Meeting locations may vary depending on the target student group and availability. For example, the first ExCEL group was conducted in a federal Trio Program, a one-stop academic service center on the University of Wisconsin-River Falls campus. The meeting was held at the Trio Program office. The second ExCEL group was conducted at residence services at NC State University. A counseling intern led the group, after receiving training from me. The residence services office was an appropriate location since the intern was also a Housing Director, and she worked with resident students. A third group was implemented through integration of a first-year seminar with four sections, in total about 75 students. The seminar is a requirement for students in the Transition Program, and most of them are from non-traditional backgrounds, with many students of color.

During the academic year, ExCEL students will also see their group advisors individually on a regular basis to discuss personal issues and difficulties. First, the advisors will find out students' strengths and weaknesses through the NCQ assessment. Focusing on their weaknesses, the advisors will help them strengthen their non-cognitive development and resolve personal problems, as well as connect the students to other academic and student services for further support and help as needed.

Students must be committed, as they are expected to attend all group meetings and meet with group leaders individually as necessary, participate in the group to share, respect and support one another in the group. Also, they are expected to complete home assignments between group meetings, and to keep confidentiality of the group issues and discussions. Finally, they will participate in the evaluation process.

Commitment from the group leader and members is also essential for successful outcomes. The roles and responsibilities of the group leader are to (a) facilitate the group sessions through discussion, role-play, simulations and etc.; (b) support group members and enhance their academic and social development; (c) review group assignments and reflecting journals and provide feedback to students; (d) counsel students one-on-one; and (e) evaluate the group process and outcomes through survey and group interviews.

In each group session, the group leader introduces the topic; handouts are distributed. Then group activities start, including discussion, role-play, games and simulations. At the end, summary and evaluation of the group session and actions are necessary to examine the outcomes of the group. Items key to thorough evaluation of group outcomes include:

- Personal profile and non-cognitive profile of students
- Changes in students' learning and study skills
- Group leader's evaluation of group success
- First year GPA of students
- Student retention rate

Themes of Group Sessions

1. Learning and study skills I
   How to survive well?
   Effective reading and listening skills, and participation in class discussion

2. Learning and study skills II
   Time management

3. Learning and study skills III
   Revision skills: summary notes, reviewing
   Improving memory

4. Developing self-appraisal system
   Reflect on current self-appraisal system
   Learn to use feedback to make changes and improvements

5. Enhancing self-concept
   Understand self and accept self
   Identify personal strengths and weakness
   Encourage for outreach and improvement

6. Improving your knowledge in a field
   Find out student's choice of major and how much they know about it
   Help students find a major
   Learn how to acquire information about a given subject/field

7. Finding a mentor/support on a campus
   What is a mentor?
   Building a mentor and mentee relationship
   How to find support on a campus?

8. Living in a multicultural community
   Understand the multicultural society
   Learn about stereotypes and presumptions in our society
   Discuss and practice ways to deal with biases

9. Getting involved in extra-curricular activities
   Introduce extra-curricular activities on campus.
   Motivate students to get involved in extra-curricular activities.
   Discuss the benefits of involving in extra-curricular activities.

10. Integration and ending a group
    Evaluation through group interview and survey

Wisconsin Group

In spring of 1994, while working as Coordinator of Advising at TRIO student support services at the University of Wisconsin-River Falls, I started the first ExCEL group experiment. The University had about 5,000 students at that time, two-thirds of the undergraduates were first-generation students and experienced an attrition rate of over 30% during students' first year. The Academic Support Office targeted first-generation, low-income students and students with disabilities, and my program enrolled about 200 students in 1994. In preparing for the ExCEL group, I met with an advisor and the Director at Multicultural Affairs Office (MAO)in order to enlist their support. The idea was to organize a group for the disadvantaged students and students of color. The Multicultural Affairs Office provided support in terms of publicizing the group, recruiting, and consultation. The ExCEL group was announced in a new student orientation of Summer, 1994, and follow-up emails were sent to invite students who were enrolled in the TRIO program and the MAO. Also, personal invitations were extended to some students through the advisor at MAO and me.

Students were invited to attend an information meeting for the ExCEL group for about 90 minutes. At the meeting, purpose, format, content, roles and evaluation about ExCEL were covered. Plenty of time was given to students for their questions. Then, at the end of the meeting, students might sign up for the group or they may choose to register later.

The group began with 11 students enrolled, including 9 females and 2 males; all but two completed the group sessions. The first drop-out occurred after the second session because of a time conflict with the student's new part-time job. Another student dropped out at the second group meeting because she had experienced a house fire. Five students of the group were Asian Americans, which reflected the fact that the largest minority group on that campus was Asian, and the rest were Caucasians. The Asian sample included 4 Hmongs and 1 Chinese. All Hmong students had immigrated with their parents to this country for at least four years and lived on campus. The Chinese student had emigrated from Hong Kong, had been a permanent resident for three years and his home was in California. The mean age was 22.3 (n=9), reflecting the four of the group members who were adult students. In the results, the ExCEL students improved their study skills, had higher GPA and retention than other students in the TRIO program (Ting, 1997b).

Residence Halls
at North Carolina State University

In 1996, another ExCEL group was organized at North Carolina State University, during second year after I became a professor in the Department of Counselor Education there. A counseling intern was interested in conducting the ExCEL group at her residence halls. A challenge for group counseling is to motivate students to join groups. However, receiving the support from

University Housing, the intern and I worked closely with the Assistant Director to set up the groups. A group of five students was recruited from a residence hall where the graduate counseling intern worked as Resident Director. We also received support from the Freshman English Program; their instructors announced the program in classes. Another group of six students were recruited from these classes. To reflect on this group experience, a key for success is to collaborate with other student services or academic programs (Ting, Grant, & Plenert, 2000).

Renewed Commitment at First Year College

The ExCEL group model has continued to receive attention. In addition to student affairs offices such as minority student services, freshman English classes, academic advising office, and housing, one of the first-year seminars was also interested in the structured group model. The Renewed Commitment Program at the First Year College, North Carolina State University was developed in response to this interest. The First Year College (FYC) at NCSU was established in 1996 with a mission to enhance student development by providing academic and social/cultural programs. FYC was designed for students who prefer a year of general study accompanied with major and career guidance. FYC believes in holistic student development and requires plenty of social and cultural programs and activities for students to enhance their academic and social integration into the new community.

Recently, two graduate counseling interns at FYC adopted the ideas and established the Renewed Commitment program. The focus of the program was to enhance academic and social support for the first-year students who were placed on academic warning at the end of the fall semester according to a student list provided by Registration and Records. FYC students with a grade point average (GPA) between 1.5 and 1.9 were identified from the list. The researchers sent letters about the program and invited them to participate. Like other EXCEL programs, an information session was held to explain the Renewed Commitment Program. A total of 28 students enrolled and completed the program. In addition to group and individual counseling, RCP also provides tutorial groups, called Success Labs. The lab provides opportunities for the students to practice their skills or strategies they learned in counseling, and tutors were available to assist students in meeting individual student goals. The program evaluation included a comparison between treatment group and control group. In the results, the RCP group had a significantly higher retention rate than the control group (Stonehouse & Ting, 2000). RCP participants' spring GPA was also slightly higher than the control group, but it did not reach statistical significance.

Transition Program

The University Transition Program (UTP) is designed to admit and support specially admitted students at an urban public university in the Southeastern U.S. The program usually admits about 60 to 70 new students every year. These students are academically under-prepared, usually having comparatively low SAT scores and high school GPAs. Students in the program are required to take a year-long seminar, to attend night time study halls, and to meet with their instructors for individual advising. The primary objective of the program is to enhance academic and personal development, and to assist participating students in finding a major. The year long seminar carries one academic credit and is designed to enhance students' cognitive-development while acquiring knowledge and advancing requisite skills for success in college. The average class size is about 15 to 20 students, and the class meets for two days a week, each for 50 minutes. Topics in the seminar include: study skills and time management, academic requirements in the different colleges of the University, enhancement of decision making skills, and challenges to engage in higher levels of thinking and reasoning.

The transition program aims to enhance specially admitted students' academic performance and retention. However, a recent study of the program indicated that the program may be ineffective in enhancing student success. Using a random sample of the UTP students (n=32), the study found that they did not obtain different mean GPAs than a control group of students (n=121), who were matched with similar high school GPAs, SAT scores, admission index, gender, age, ethnicity, and types of housing. Therefore, the program began to consider how to revise the curriculum and teaching methods to increase the effectiveness of the first-year seminar.

The UTP director consulted me and learnt about the ExCEL program. Then he decided to incorporate the non-cognitive strategies (Sedlacek, 2004), and adopt the ExCEL program (Ting, 1999) into the UTP curriculum. The UTP used a group approach for the class.

Instructors of the UTP received training in using the ExCEL group approach and the new curriculum. Students met twice a week in a group facilitated class, each for 50 minutes. Students were expected to attend the classes, to participate in the group activities, to respect and to support one another in the groups, to complete home assignments, to attend one-on-one advising bi-weekly, to attend tutorials at the evening study hall, and to participate in the evaluation. In addition to ExCEL expectations, ExCEL topics were adopted into the class. Assignments included writing essays on goals for college life, personal biography, and reflections on in-class experiences. Students were also required to attend a computer workshop and to conduct a library search based on a worksheet. In the spring, other topics included getting involved in extracurricular activities, a community service project, peers relationship, decision making, and moral reasoning.

Chapter 5:
Non-Cognitive Assessment
for Group Members

Sedlacek (1998) proposed the Non-Cognitive Variable Model for student assessment. The term noncognitive is used "[to refer] to variables relating to adjustments, motivation, and perceptions, rather than traditional variables and quantitative (often called cognitive) areas typically measured by standardized tests" (Sedlacek, 2004, p. 36). Tracey and Sedlacek (1984, 1989) designed the Non-Cognitive Questionnaire (NCQ) to assess psychosocial aspects of students that influence college success. The NCQ contains 23 items: 18 Likert-formatted, two multiple choice, and three open-ended. The instrument assesses eight variables with possible score ranges printed within the following parentheses: (a) positive self-concept (7-27): students demonstrate confidence, strength of character, determination, and independence; (b) realistic self-appraisal (4-14): students recognize and accept any strengths and deficiencies, especially academic, work hard at self-development; and recognize need to broaden their individuality; (c) demonstrated community service (2-8): students participate and are involved in their community; (d) knowledge acquired in a field (2-8): students acquire knowledge in a sustained or culturally way in any field; (e) successful leadership experience (3-13): students demonstrate strong leadership in any area of their background such as religious groups, sports, and student clubs; (f) preference for long-range goals (3-13): students are able to respond to deferred gratification, set goals and plan for their future; (g) ability to understand and cope with racism (5-25): students exhibit a realistic view of the system on the basis of personal experiences of racism; are committed to improving existing system, and can handle racism, and (h) availability of a strong support person (3-15): students seek and take advantages a strong support network or have someone to turn to when needed (Sedlacek, 2004).

The students respond to items related to their high school experiences in classes, extra-curricular activities, and their respective communities. Other questions assess their motivation, self-confidence, and future goals. A scoring key was developed combining a 5-point scale (1 for strongly disagree and 5 for strongly agree) for the 18 Likert-formatted items and a rating guideline for the 3 open-ended items for the scales of Long-Term Goals, Knowledge Acquired in a Field, Successful Leadership Experience, and Demonstrated Community Services. The validity and reliability of the NCQ are well established (Tracey & Sedlacek, 1984, 1985, 1987, 1989). Correlation coefficients for internal consistency of the NCQ scales were over .80, construct validity was reported by a factor analysis (Tracey & Sedlacek, 1989), and predictive ability was reported in many studies such as Tracey and Sedlacek (1984, 1985), Sedlacek (2004), and Ting and Robinson (1998) (See Table 5.1 for a description of the non-cognitive variables and Appendix One for the Non-Cognitive Questionnaire; NCQ).

Table 5.1 Description of Non-Cognitive Variables

1. Positive Self-concept

    Successful individuals expressed confidence in their ability to achieve the goal of graduating regardless of the obstacles that may arise. Individuals expected to do well in both academic and non-academic arenas and made positive statements about themselves and assumed that they were able to handle any challenges that may come their way. There was a high level of self-efficacy and self-esteem, always positive looking into the future.

2. Realistic Self-appraisal

    Individuals were able to recognize and accept background academic deficiencies and values working toward personal development. They also appreciated and understood the rewards as well as the consequences of different levels of individual performance and developed an effective feedback interpretation system. They did not overreact or personalize criticism or rewards but saw them as logical consequences of performance, even though evaluations can be biased.

3. Understands and Deals with Racism

    Individuals had a realistic view of racism based on personal experience and understood the role of the "system" in their life and how it arbitrarily treats minority individuals. Individuals had developed a method of assessing the system and were responsive according to the cultural or racial demands it places on them. Similarly, individuals were able to evaluate the gains from responding to situational and institutionalized racism and did not blame others for their own struggles but were not blind to injustice, either.

4. Prefers Long-range to Short-term or Immediate Needs

    Individuals could set goals and work towards them for a significant amount of time without reinforcement. They were able to exhibit patience and experience partial fulfillment of a longer-term goal in small steps. Individuals had a future and a past orientation allowing them to look past the immediate situation and had insight into the benefits of planning for academic and non-academic goals. They were willing to sacrifice immediate needs for achieving a long range goal.

5. Availability of a Strong Support Person

    Individuals were able to recognize when they needed help and were willing to ask for it. They may have had one or more specifically identified mentors or friends who provided support and encouragement on a regular basis. Individuals also recognized the difficulties inherent in being a "loner" and rarely relied solely on their own resources to address problems.

6. Successful Leadership Position
    Individuals have had experience in leadership positions and have experienced influencing and assisting others in both academic and non-academic situations. They were comfortable providing directions and advice to others and had experience mediating in disputes and disagreements between peers. Similarly, they had no problem taking appropriate action when a situation called for it.

7. Demonstrated Community Service
    Individuals had identified with a cultural and/or racial group that has had a specific and long-term relationship within the community. Similarly, the individual had a history of involvement in community-based activities and/or organizations that have accomplished specific goals in the community setting.

8. Knowledge Acquired in a Field
    Individuals had a non-traditional and possible culturally and/or racially based interest and experiential knowledge regarding a field or area that had not been formally studied in school. They had also developed innovative and creative ways in which to acquire information about a particular area.

(Adapted from Sedlacek, 1987 pp. 485)

Tracey and Sedlacek (1984) reported a 2-week test-retest reliability of a range from .74 to .94, with a median of .85 for the NCQ items. Interrater reliability on the three open-ended NCQ items ranged from .73 to 1.00. Interrater reliability is generally recorded at .80 and above in other studies (Boyer & Sedlacek, 1988; Hood, 1992; Ting & Robinson, 1998; Ting, 2001).

The NCQ appears to have strong content validity and construct and predictive validity. Ting and Robinson (1998) concluded that the non-cognitive variables predicted academic performance and student retention effectively for the following student populations: Asian Americans, African Americans, Hispanics, Caucasians, specially admitted students, and low-income and first-generation students. Correlations with college grades and retention were significantly higher when non-cognitive variables were used in conjunction with standardized test scores and earlier grades.

Use of the Noncognitive Questionnaire in Universities

There are currently a number of examples of the successful adoption of the NCQ for college and university admissions, programs, and services. For example, since adopting the NCQ in the admissions process at the Louisiana State

University Medical School, minority student enrollment has doubled to 21% with an 87% retention rate (Sedlacek, 1998). Eighty percent of admissions committee members reported that they believed using non-cognitive variables in making admission decisions was worthwhile. North Carolina State University adapted items from NCQ for supplementary information in its undergraduate application package, e.g. leadership experiences, community services and educational aspirations. Muhlenberg College, a 1,800-student liberal arts college in Allentown, Pennsylvania, also collects applicant information about leadership in extra-curricular activities and community service. As an option, the college allows the applicants not to report SAT or ACT scores.

NCQ data have also been used to devise strategies for intervention programs and services in universities. For example, Sedlacek (1991) reported such data's effectiveness in assessing students' psychosocial development for individual counseling. Ting, Grant and Plenert (2000) found NCQ indicators useful in assessing and enhancing students' psychosocial adjustment in on-going groups. Also, Fogleman and Saeger (1985) reported a successful application in a summer enrichment program for health majors.

The NCQ has been used in other ways. Gates Millennium Scholars Program adopts the NCQ to assess applications: applicants' essays are scored, by specially trained scorers, according to noncognitive variables.

Administration and Scores Profiles

The NCQ can be administered in several ways (Sedlacek, 2004). Firstly, the NCQ can be handed out as questionnaires at the new student orientation. Usually, this method can college most responses from the freshmen because majority of them will attend new student orientation. Group leaders who receive the NCQ and instructions for administration may distribute the questionnaires to students in groups. A second method is to college applicants responses in the application process by including the NCQ in application packets. Like new student orientation, typically most applicants will complete and return the NCQ. Thirdly, for an ExCEL group, typically, the group leader will administer the NCQ during the first session. Based on the results of the NCQ, group leaders can help interpret the scores to the students. Also, students may learn more about their results by comparing their scores to the norms (See Sedalcek, 2004) or to the following profile:

	High Score	Low Score
1.POSTIVE SELF-CONCEPT OR CONFIDENCE	Feels confident in making it through graduation. Makes positive statements about him/herself. Expects to do well in academic and non-academic areas. Assumes he/she can handle new situations or challenges.	Not sure he/she has ability to do well in college. Feels other students are better than he/she is. Expects to get marginal grades. Feels he/she will have trouble balancing personal and academic life. Avoids new challenges or situations.

2. REALISTIC SELF APPRAISAL	Appreciates and accepts rewards as well as consequences of poor performance. Understands that reinforcement is imperfect, and does not overreact to positive or negative feedback. Has developed a system of using feedback to alter behavior.	Not sure how evaluations are done in school. Overreacts to most recent reinforcement (positive or negative), rather than seeing it in a larger context. Does not know how he/she is doing in class until grades are out. Does not have a good idea of how peers would rate his/her performance.
3. LIVING IN A MULTICULTURAL SOCIETY	Has a realistic view of the multicultural society based on personal experience and understood the role of different socio-political systems impacting his/her life and how it arbitrarily treats minority individuals. Has developed a sense of awareness of diverse cultures and accept people from different racial cultural backgrounds. In addition, the person has made friends, worked with these people and can live with them in society in harmony.	Not sure how the "system" works. Preoccupied with racism or does not feel racism exists. Blames others for problems. Reacts with the same intensity to large and small issues concerned with race/culture. Does not have a method of successfully handling racism that does not interfere with personal and academic development.
4. PREFERS LONG-RANGE TO SHORT-TERM OR IMMEDIATE NEEDS	Can set goals and proceed for some time without reinforcement. Shows patience. Can see partial fulfillment of a longer term goal. Is future and past oriented, and does not just see immediate issues or problems. Shows evidence of planning in academic and non-academic areas.	Lack of evidence of setting and accomplishing goals. Likely to proceed without clear direction. Relies on other to determine outcomes. Lives in present. Does not have a "plan" for approaching a course, school in general, an activity, etc. Goals, when stated, are vague and unrealistic.
5. AVAILABILITY OF STRONG SUPPORT PERSON	Has identified and received help, support, and encouragement from one or more specific individuals. Does not rely solely on his/her own resources to solve problems. Is not a "loner". Willing to admit that he/she needs help when appropriate.	No evidence of turning to others for help. No single support person, mentor, or close advisor can be identified. Does not talk about his/her problems. Feels he/she can handle things on his/her own. Access to previous support person may be reduced or eliminated. Is not aware of the importance of a support person.

6. SUCCESSFUL LEADERSHIP EXPERIENCE	Has shown evidence of influencing others in academic and non-academic areas. Comfortable providing advice and direction to others. Has served as mediator in disputes or disagreements among colleagues. Comfortable in taking action where called for.	No evidence that others turn to him/her for advice or direction. Non-assertive. Does not take initiative. Overly cautious. Avoid controversy. Not well known by peers.
7. DEMONSTRATED COMMUNITY SERVICE	Identifies with a group which is cultural, racial, and/or geographic. Has specific and long-term relationships in a community. Has been active in community activities over a period of time. Has accomplished specific goals in a community setting.	No involvement in cultural, racial or geographical group or community. Limited activities of any kind. Fringe member of group(s). Engages more in solitary rather than group activities (academic or non-academic).
8. KNOWLEDGE ACQUIRED IN A FIELD	Knows about a field or area that he/she has formally studied in school. Has a non-traditional, possibly culturally or racially-biased view of a field. Has developed innovative ways to acquire new information about a given subject or field.	Appears to know little about or areas he/she has not studied in school. No evidence of learning from community or non-academic activities. Traditional in approach to learning. Has not received credit-by-exam.

Table: 5.2 High and Low Scores Profile of NCQ
Adapted from Sedlacek (2007)

ExCEL Group leaders focus on strengths and weaknesses in a follow-up meeting with each student. Then, the leader designs a plan for enhancing the student's weak areas.

Another form of evaluation uses short-answer questions. The screening process for Gates Millennium Scholars Program, a $1 billion grant for financial aid for college bound students of color, has modified the NCQ into a series of short questions (Sedlacek, 2004). These short-answer items compare how applicants score with information provided on their personal statements, letters of recommendations, and other parts of the application. In order to achieve score reliability, raters were trained to identify and consider non-cognitive dimensions. Then, reliability of ratings was calculated (above .90).

Portfolios are another way to explore students' non-cognitive dimensions. Faculty evaluators were trained in evaluating applicants' portfolios using the non-cognitive profiles of high and low scores (See Table 5.2).

Essays can be assessed with non-cognitive variables, as well. For example, the aforementioned Gates Millennium Scholars Program adopted the non-cognitive variables to assess applicants' essays with an inter-rater correlation coefficient of .81 (Sedlacek, 2004). Studies are under way to relate those scores to academic and nonacademic outcomes such as academic persistence, retention, and grades.

Non-Cognitive Questionnaire-Revised 2

One of the challenges for the NCQ is that there are 3 open-ended items, and it can take more time to compose the score. In a later study (Ting & Sedlacek, 2000), NCQ-R2, a revised version of the NCQ was studied with promising results.

Table 5.3: Additional Factors Found from NCQ-R 2

Factors	High Scores	Low Scores
1. HIGH SCHOOL COURSE WORK	Has studied a variety of courses in high school above and beyond its requirements. Interested in studying/ preparing for universities and unafraid of taking difficult demanding courses.	Has tried to avoid demanding and advanced level courses in high school. Instead, S/he tends to take basic requirements. May not have planned to attend university.
2. MOTIVATION TO STUDY	Expresses specific interests in attending college. Is, as a consequence, more internally-driven and are motivated in learning. Usually not limited in one or two disciplines, showing instead a wide range of academic interests.	Not motivated well to study and may display behaviors such as skipping classes and tardiness. Cannot concentrate in studying. They are not sure about their future careers.
3. STUDYING METHOD AND EFFECTIVENESS	Has an effective studying method, is more concentrated in studying and has maintained a regular and consistent studying pattern. Usually, these individuals are better prepared for tests and examinations.	Displays poor studying method and tries to procrastinate. Usually regards studying method as less effective and tends to cram before tests.
4. EXPECTATION OF INVOLVEMENT WITH FACULTY	Has had a good relationship with teachers and likes to interact with faculty. Believes that he/she can benefit from such experiences for personal and career development. Would seek help from academic support services if needed.	Has not developed a close relationship with high school teachers. These individuals do not believe that professors can help their personal and career development. Thus, they tend not to seek help from professors.

5. EMOTIONAL INTELLIGENCE	Aware of own feelings and is popular for taking care of others' emotional needs. Can continue to work well under stresses from the environment or in an unfavorable situation.	Can be affected by their emotions and does not have a good relationship with his/her friends. Cannot deal with stresses and emotions so well as those who scores higher on this scale.

In 2000, the NCQ was modified into NCQ-Revised 2 (Ting & Sedlacek, 2000), a multiple-choice, 68-item instrument. New factors believed to be measured by the questionnaire were confirmed: (1) High school coursework: Students who complete vigorous high school courses and are academically prepared for universities; (2) Motivation to study: Students are internally-driven and are motivated in learning; (3) Study method and effectiveness: Students have effective study skills and can work independently; (4) Expected involvement with faculty: Students expect to work with professors and are interested in getting help from academic support services; and (5) Emotional intelligence: Students can maintain a balance with their emotions and can work under pressure or a unfavorable environment (See Appendix Two NCQ-R2).

Chapter 6:
ExCEL Group Process—Study Skills

Study skills are vitally important for success in the first year of college. Studies show that study skills are related moderately to academic performance. Nisbet & Watkins (1986) found that the learning styles of students were good predictors of their grades and retention, and an increase in the predictable GPA variance of approximately 11% was obtained by including the Myers-Briggs Types Indicator and Effective Study Skills Test in a support program (Nisbet, Ruble & Schurr, 1982). Academically struggling college students (GPA lower than 2.5) were found to be weaker in seven of ten areas from the Learning and Study Strategies Inventory (LASSI; Weinstein & Palmer, 2002) than their normal-achieving counterparts (GPA above 2.5) (Proctor, Prevatt, Adams, Hurst, & Petscher, 2006). Areas that coincided with academic problems were Anxiety, Concentration, Information Processing, Motivation, Selecting Main Ideas, Time Management, and Test Strategies.

Note-taking was found to be the best predictor of total course performance and critical thinking was the strongest predictor for multiple-choice-examination performance among 292 college students over two semesters (Williams & Worth, 2002). Outline format may be the most common form of note taking (Flippo & Caverly, 2000). Matrices integrate relationships within and across topics. Compared to matrices, the outline format targets both primary and secondary points within topics, whereas Armbruster's (2000) review of the note taking literature concluded that the outline format offers retrieval cues for later reviewing.

In the ExCEL Group, the first part of the group sessions is devoted to study skills. Topics covered are: (a) general study skills, reading skills and note-taking skills in the classroom, (b) time management, and (c) preparing for tests/examinations, including improving memory.

Session One: Building the Relationship and Basic Study Skills

In the first session, the main goal is to introduce the ExCEL group and allow the students to get acquainted with one another. To begin, the group leader introduces one or two ice-breaking activities. Then, the leader discusses the ground rules for the group, which may include: respecting and supporting others, participation in group meetings and activities, confidentiality of group materials, and avoiding negative criticism. Also, the students share their personal objectives of attending the group. After ice-breakers, the first content topic is introduced, and the group leader begins to discuss study skills. Study skills content focus is how to get the most from classes: listening and note taking skills.

EXCEL GROUP
SESSION 1
BUILD THE RELATIONSHIP AND
BASIC STUDY SKILLS

Objectives:
1. Introduce the group to students.
2. Students will get to know one another.
3. Discuss personal objectives and ground rules.
4. Introduce basic study skills.
5. Ask the students to complete the Noncognitive Questionnaire and the Learning and Study Strategies Inventory

Procedures:
I. Introduction and ice-breaker - 15 minutes

II. Ground rules - 20 minutes
   The group leader discusses ground rules with group members

III. Personal objectives - 10 minutes
   All group members share about their personal objectives in attending this group.

IV. How to learn well in classes? – Reading and listening skills - 40 minutes
   - before class
   - during class
   - after class

V. Assignments - 5 minutes
   Leader will explain the assignments and ask students to complete them at home.
   1. Complete Noncongitive Questionnaire, Learning and Study Strategies Inventory (LASSI).
   2. Report how you use the skills in the next meeting.
   3. Record your next week's activities and time use. Bring your class timetable and weekly activities log to the next meeting.

The leader leads a discussion about how to get the most from a class/lecture. Topics include reading skills, effective listening and note taking. In addition, reading skills such as SQ3R are covered:

- Firstly, Survey the chapter quickly by glancing over the main points. Ask the following questions: What is the purpose of the reading material? Focus on titles, chapter objectives, introduction and conclusion, first and last statement of a paragraph, pictures, and highlighted words.

- Ask questions in the second reading. Turn the headings and subheadings into questions. Also, ask yourself: "how do these questions relate to what I have learned/know from the class or a previous lesson/chapter?"
- Thirdly, read to find out answers. Try to find answers from the reading by focusing on the questions written earlier. Develop charts, graphs, or tables to help understand difficult concepts/theories.
- Fourthly, try to tell the main points of a section by reciting. Ask yourself what you just read and learned by restating the main points through reciting them aloud, writing them down, or a combination of both.
- Finally, review the chapter again to make sure you understand and grasp the main points. Reorganize your notes for the chapter or develop a study guide, flashcards, and practice quizzes. Compare class notes and reading materials, as well, to enrich your review.

In addition to reading skills, suggestions for taking lecture notes are discussed in the ExCEL group meeting (Mundsack, Deese, & Deese, 2002):

- Listen actively by thinking and engaging in the lecture or instructions.
- Preview the chapter or assigned reading before class or a lecture. Write down questions and look for answers from the lecture/class.
- In class, try to structure the lecture as the students are listening. Pay attention to what the instructor tries to emphasize.
- Take notes while listening to the lecture.
- After class, compare your notes with the textbook.
- Review the points/sections where there are any disconnections or gaps between the textbook and the notes.
- The sooner you review after the lecture, the more efficient, also the better you can understand and remember what you've learned.

The assignments for this session include completing the Noncongitive Questionnaire and Learning and Study Strategies Inventory (LASSI), practicing the new study skills and reporting experiences in the in the next meeting, and recording next week's activities and time use.

Session Two: Time Management

In the second session, the leader begins to discuss time management with the goal of improving students' study skills. Self-monitoring (Cormier & Nurius, 2003), a skill essential for effective studying and for self-improvement in general, is introduced in this session by discussing personal time management choices. At the end of the first session, the students are asked to observe and record their own particular behavior (thoughts, feelings and actions) in the following week and interactions with environmental events, for example, a sports match, part-time work, and a party. Were they attracted by a sports match on TV and did not work on their homework? Did they go to a party with friends and forget about studying? Did they need to work so much that they did not have enough time to study? In the first session, they are asked to bring a weekly record to the next ExCEL group meeting for discussion. At the group meeting, the students work with the group leader to improve their weekly schedule. They are asked to insert stimulus between major blocks of study/work time and to self-reward for successfully following a new daily activity schedule. Such stimulus exercises stimulus control—the act of prearranging antecedents or cues to increase or decrease a client's performance of a target behavior—and self-reward—giving clients themselves a positive stimulus following a desired response (Corminer & Nurius, 2003). For example, the group leader encourages the students to develop a habit of working on homework immediately when they turn on their computers instead of browsing around websites or checking email, so that the stimulus of the computer is equated with study, not internet surfing. In order to self-reward, students might give themselves a five-minute break after each one-hour studying block. After learning these new behaviors, the students are asked to record their activities in the coming week and to share their experience in the next group meeting. Through this activity, students learn to reflect upon their current time management and to learn new skills to better use their time.

In practice, students were amazed when they found that much time was unorganized or "dead": time on the phone, playing computer/TV games, on-line chatting, chatting with roommates, or just idling. Some students had a heavy part-time job, over 20 hours per week. Others were not motivated to study after class while they were sitting in their residence halls. In the ExCEL group, other interesting issues were found such as time wasters. Time wasters are idling time, or non-productive hours, usually occurred when students do not plan well how to use their time or they are not concentrated on their work. Other time wasters included stress, anxiety, procrastination, lack of planning, and bad habits. On the average, the students had little time to study on a regular basis. Through discussions in the ExCEL group, new strategies were raised to tackle time management problems. Here's a list of the strategies:
- schedule regular study time
- break down study time into blocks
- create incentives for blocks of study time
- use "dead" hours well, e.g. study in the library instead of sitting in the cafeteria
- find a permanent quiet study place (such as in the library)
- plan specific time for emails and online chatting (for example, during a break)
- reduce part-time work
- prioritize the items (or work)
- work on easier tasks first, if possible
- do not procrastinate

In results, students reported improvements in time management after implementing these new strategies.

EXCEL GROUP
SESSION 2
TIME MANAGEMENT

Objectives:
1. Students will understand the concepts of time management.
2. Students will recognize the importance of time management.
3. Students will design their own study schedules.
4. Students will practice using these schedules.

Procedures:
I. Review of session one and students' activities in the past week- 10 minutes

II. Better time management
 - What are your personal challenges/problems for time management? - 20 minutes
 - A typical example - 5 minutes
 - Why make a schedule - 5 minutes
 - Scheduling principles - 5 minutes
 - Stimulus control and self reward – 5 minutes
 - Types of Schedule: Weekly and semester – 10 minutes
 - Working out a weekly schedule - 20 minutes

IV. Summary and assignment - 5 minutes
 - Complete your weekly studying schedule at home
 - Practice the schedules and report the results in next meeting:
   Encourage students to make efforts to try and to report their difficulties.

Session Three: Revision and Test Preparation

In session 3, the ExCEL group completes the topic on study skills by focusing on revision and test preparation, including improving memory. For group discussion, the group leader has prepared some tips for revision and test preparation:
- Prepare some questions and ask the instructor/classmates.
- Review the notes and fill in missing points or confused concepts from text or other sources.
- Edit notes taken from classes; highlight the key points with different colors.
- Develop tables, charts, figures to compare theories, concepts, applications, and limitations.
- Review the notes and materials developed before tests/examinations.

- Join a study group.
- Attend tutorials.
- Practice by taking previous tests, if available; then focus on studying weak areas.
- Make sure you have enough rest and sleep, and maintain a balanced lifestyle.

EXCEL GROUP
SESSION 3
REVISION AND TEST PREPARATION

Objectives:
1. Students will learn about revision and test preparation skills.
2. Students will use these skills in their studies.

Procedures
I. Reports and feedback from last meeting - 10 minutes

II. Revision skills - 40 minutes
   - Reviewing principles: reduce, recite, reflect and review
     (1) Reduce: Use tables, charts, figures, flow-charts and pictures to summarize/compare
     (2) Recite: Read, read aloud and write many times.
     (3) Reflect: Ask questions.
     (4) Review: Refresh by studying again periodically.

   - Test preparation:
     Discuss test preparation skills

III. Suggestions about how to improve memory -- 30 minutes
   Including the power of mnemonic devices

IV. Feedback and home assignments -- 10 minutes
   Tell students to practice the related skills and bring some examples to next group meeting.

In order to have an effective revision, it is suggested that students strengthen their concentration by developing a positive attitude towards study, organizing their notes and study materials, asking more questions, and giving self reward for good performance. Meanwhile, they should avoid a noisy environment, idling, or too many sidetracks. The students may improve their concentration if they can find a consistent location in which to study, maintain a regular study schedule, develop studying blocks with a variety of different subjects, talk to themselves to help concentrate, develop a task list, and use more senses (e.g. writing and thinking or drawing and reciting).

When striving to improve memory, it is important to explore an individual's memory style, which is directly related to learning style. A test developed by Feldman (2007) can be adopted to determine dominant memory style: verbal, auditory, or kinesthetic. The test asks students to choose their learning preference in different situations such as at a class, learning how to dance, recalling a memory, and remembering a complex procedure. Answers imply trends in learning choices and memory style.

After finding out a memory style, how can students improve their memory? The principles are organizing study materials and using their minds and bodies. Spending time to organize their notes into charts, tables, figures, and diagrams, will greatly enhance memory. Also, in the process, learners use their minds and bodies together, which can increase memory as well. Other memory skills include: mnemonics, "chunking", rehearsal, key words, and story or picture telling (Feldman, 2007). Mnemonics are techniques which organize materials in a specific structure or pattern to stimulate/enhance memory. Acronyms, for instance, are words or phrases formed by the first letters of a series of words/terms: EU stands for European Union, LD for learning disorder, and ExCEL group stands for Excellent Commitment and Effective Learning group. Acrostics are the first letters in a sentence made from words or materials which need to be remembered; Every Body Loves Him might help a learner recall the sequence for a series of concepts, "Empathy, Bonding, Love, and Happiness," My Friends Call Me Funny helps students remember how grammar should work, "Memories, Facts, Concepts, Mechanical, and Format." "Chunking" is grouping facts together in a meaningful way: for example, starting to remember the lowest level concepts of a theory first. Rehearsing is practicing by writing, drawing, and talking. This may include self testing by writing down the key concepts or a conceptual diagram. Story telling or picture drawing is especially effective for individuals who prefer visual memory. Students memorize by organizing the study materials into a story or a picture. Then, they may recall it by re-telling the details of the story or the picture.

Chapter 7: ExCEL Group Process—Non-Cognitive Topics

The focus for the group is adjustment. Psychosocial development is a key to adjustment to college life (Sedlacek, 2004; Ting & Robinson, 1998; Tinto, 1993). Therefore, psychosocial topics are the core of the ExCEL group: developing a self-appraisal system, enhancing one's self-concept, improving knowledge in a field, living in a diverse community, finding a mentor/support person, and involvement in co-curricular/community activities.

Session Four: Realistic Self-Appraisal System

In the fourth group session, the leader begins to introduce the non-cognitive topics. In this session, the focus is improving students' self-appraisal systems. Open-ended questions and reframing are used to help students to understand their studying problems and to encourage them to use a different view to appraise their own performance (Cormier & Nurius, 2003). Students are challenged through conversation, reflection on items in a form, and group interaction to identify, understand, and reframe their perspectives on their academic situations. First, the group leader uses a series of open-ended questions; here's an excerpt from a group session:

Group leader: Are you aware of the evaluation/grading method of your classes? Can you share some examples?

Student A: Oh yes, I know that my psychology professor is pretty strict on grading. He designed a grading system including many things like quizzes, tests, case study, journals, and papers.

Student B: I am not quite sure about this. I just know that I am doing ok in my class.

Student C: I am taking five classes now, some classes are more difficult, like English and mathematics. But I am not sure about my grades now.

Group Leader: It sounds like some of you know the grading systems in your classes and some others are not as sure. Is it important to know how you are graded?

(later in the same group session)

Group Leader: How do you evaluate your own performance in classes, then?

Student A: I am always looking for at least a "B" from classes.

Student B: I am not sure, as long as I can learn something. Then it is fine.

Student C: Well, it varies, and it depends on which classes. If I like the class, like tennis, I enjoy it and want to do more. If I don't like it, like English, I am not going to do a lot or expect a good grade anyway.

Group leader: Ok, what if you do not do well in a class? Have you had this experience?

(Students will share related experiences and the leader will help them process the experiences and find out the reasons for outcomes. Group focus is on how they appraise their performance, self-adjust and improve in classes in which they are not doing well.)

The group leader continues to challenge the student to think from alternative perspectives about their self-evaluation system. Other questions may be used, e.g., "How do you study for this class?" "How do you know if the studying methods are effective?" "Did you try other studying methods?" Finally, when the student begins to change his or her perspectives, more open-ended questions are used to help him or her explore from a reframed perspective, with general questions first, such as "How might you improve your performance?" Then, more specific questions are asked to help the student develop a new perspective, including, "What are the resources or help you can get on campus or from your family, friends, etc for your studying?" "How do you respond to advice or feedback from a friend or your major advisor?" At the end of the session, the group leader will ask the students to summarize what they have learned from the session. The homework is to practice these changes in their classes and share the new experiences in the next session.

**ExCEL GROUP
SESSION 4
REALISTIC SELF-APPRAISAL SYSTEM**

Objectives:
1. Students will review their current self-appraisal system.
2. Students will learn to use feedback to improve themselves.
3. Students will improve their self-appraisal system.

Procedures;
I. Review of last meeting - 5 minutes
II. Form groups of twos - 20 minutes
   - Tell one another about your current classes.
   - Tell one another about classes you like most and least and why.
   - Report when the group reunites.
III. Whole group discussion - 60 minutes
   1. Are you aware of the evaluation/grading methods of your classes? Give two examples.
   2. How do you evaluate your performance in classes? What are the guidelines or criteria you use? Give an example.
   3. Share about a class in which you are not doing well, comparatively. How do you explain the reasons for this?
   4. How do you study for this class? How may you improve your approach?

> 5. What resources or help can you get on campus or from your family, friends, etc for studying?
> 6. How do you respond to advice or feedback from a friend? What about from your major advisor?
> 7. Summarize what you have learned from the above questions and activities.
>
> IV. Home assignment – 5 minutes
> Complete the worksheet which reflects your self-appraisal skills.

Session Five: Positive Self-Concept

In the fifth session, the ExCEL group topic is developing a positive self-concept. The objectives for the session are to help students understand themselves, identify their strengths and weaknesses, and to become more aware of who they are. Guided imagery is adopted in this session. Guided imagery is used to address a wide range of problems, including changing feelings and emotions related to anxiety, migraine, physical problems, allergies, and grieving (Corminer & Nurius, 2003). In guided imagery, a person focuses on positive thoughts or images while imaging a discomforting or anxiety-arousing activity or situation (Corimer & Nurius, 2003; Meichenbaum, 1977). By focusing on positive and pleasant images, the person is able to "block" the painful, fearful, or anxiety–provoking situation.

In the ExCEL group, members focus on examining and enhancing their self confidence in an image fantasy of themselves as blooming flowers. The guided imagery consists of a few steps. After explaining the imagery exercises to the students, the leader asks the students to relax through a breathing exercise to help them quiet down and clear their mind. Then, the leader guides the students into an image journey of becoming a rose. S/he asks the students to pay attention to the details of the flower such as height, color, location, and surroundings. Next, the leader asks the students to change their images into walking on a beach. S/he asks the students to pick up an empty jar and write down three things about which they are presently worried, then to throw the jar away, into the sea. Finally, the leader helps the students process their feelings and thinking in relation to self-concept. The rose symbolizes individual self-perceptions and the jar with notes represents their anxieties now. This exercise helps the students become more self-aware and encourages them to be more self-confident (see the following table for detailed procedure).

In practice, most of the students could imagine themselves as roses and were able to write down their worries. They appreciated the exercise, which they thought powerfully revealed their self images and anxieties. Many of them were able to focus on the weak areas of their self-concept and worries and worked with the leader in individual sessions to improve on these areas. Sometimes, a student cannot have images during the exercise. The leader should ask him/her to come and talk individually as a follow-up.

EXCEL GROUP
SESSION 5
POSITIVE SELF-CONCEPT

Objectives:
1. Students will understand more who they are.
2. Students will identify their personal strengths and weaknesses.
3. Students will become more aware of who they are.

Procedures
I. Review of last meeting - 10 minutes
II. Rose journey - 20 minutes

Objective: To allow students to work imaginatively in order to reflect their self images.

Steps:
1. Relaxation: Sit in a relaxed position, breathe slowly, and relax your body slowly (one at a time): head, neck, shoulder and upper body; arm, hands, legs, feet and ankles.

2. Imagine you are a flower, describe the flower (you):
   - What type of flower is it?
   - Describe how it grows.
   - Focus on the flower and describe how it opens up.
   - Describe how it stands: its height, color, and other features.
   - Describe the surroundings: Any plants near you? How do they grow?
   - Describe the background: Where is the flower located? Describe it.

3. Now imagine you are walking alone on a beach which is quiet and empty:
   - The breeze is blowing on your face. Feel the breeze; How do you feel?
   - You find a jar in the sands. You kneel down and pick it up. The jar is empty.
   - Now write 3 things about your current anxieties/worries on a piece of paper.
   - What are the three things?
   - Put the piece of paper in the jar.
   - Use your whole strength to throw the jar into the sea
   - You can see the jar drifting off, and it becomes smaller until it disappears.
   - The piece of paper is gone now. How do you feel now?

4. In your own time, you may open your eyes.

5. Process the Rose Journey in your group; focus on the relationship between the self and the flower

> III. A Review about You - 60 minutes
>   Discuss with students about how they evaluate their own selves.
>   Examples of topics for discussion:
>   personal strengths and weaknesses, self image, ethnic/racial identity development
>
> IV. Assignments: Complete the table about self-concept.

Session Six: Improving Your Ways to Study in A Field

In the sixth session, the group topic is improving learning and knowledge in a field. Often, this learning may come in nontraditional ways; literature shows the predictive value of non-traditional learning for academic success for different student groups such as: African Americans (Tracey & Sedlacek, 1984; 1985; 1987; 1988, 1989); Hispanics (Fuertes & Sedlcek, 1994); international students (Boyer & Sedlacek, 1988); special program students (Ting, 1997); women (Sedlacek, 1997), and engineering students (Ting, 2001). Nontraditional means of learning may include volunteering in the community, social groups, becoming involved in religious activities, and part-time work.

In this group session, the group leader encourages the students to improve their learning and knowledge in a field. In the beginning, the group leader hands out a worksheet, the Name Three Game (see the table below) and asks the students to complete the worksheet. Then, s/he will lead a discussion on how to make improvements.

> **The Name Three Game**
>
> Instructions: Provide three names in your field/major in the following items:
>
> Professional associations 1. _____
>
>   2. _____
>
>   3. _____
>
> Books other than texts 1. _____
>
>   2. _____
>
>   3. _____
>
> The "big names" in your field 1. _____ 2. _____ 3. _____

Names of instructors	1. _____	2. _____	3. _____
Office hours of instructors	1. _____	2. _____	3. _____
Where to find jobs	1. _____	2. _____	3. _____
The "hot issues"	1. _____	2. _____	3. _____
Skills required	1. _____	2. _____	3. _____
Course sequence	1. _____	2. _____	3. _____
Top three schools	1. _____	2. _____	3. _____
On-campus/off campus services or activities	1. _____	2. _____	3. _____

In practice, the students found the worksheet very useful. They were amazed that they were unaware of much information related to their fields. Some did not know the requirements of their degree programs, and others had not yet contacted their advisors/professors outside of the classroom. Many did not know the top three schools or the hot topics in their fields. Students new to the university community and its reliance on "networking" were therefore able to learn from the session about ways to improve their learning and knowledge in a field. See the following table for the details of group procedures.

EXCEL GROUP
SESSION 6
IMPROVING YOUR WAYS TO STUDY IN A FIELD

Objectives:
. Students will examine their knowledge about how to study in an academic discipline.
. Students will discuss ways to improve this knowledge.

Procedures:
Review of last meeting - 5 minutes

I. Students complete the worksheet, the Name Three Game – 10 minutes

II. Discuss the responses on the worksheet – 20 minutes

V. Discussion: How can you increase your learning and knowledge in your field – 30 minutes
Students break into groups of twos or threes and discuss the following

topics in relation to how to increase their knowledge from these sources. Students record the discussion and report the summary to the whole group.
  a. Yourself
  b. Faculty/Advisors
  c. Peer Groups
  d. On-campus Services/Activities
  e. Off-Campus Services/Activities
  f. Others (e.g. professional associations).

V. Summary and assignment – 10 minutes
- Complete the worksheet: "How to increase your knowledge in a field."
- Start to look for mentor and report progress to the group in the next meeting.

Session Seven: Find A Mentor

In the seventh group session, the theme is mentoring or a support person. Literature shows many benefits of mentoring: providing more career/academic development, better psychosocial functions, and more counseling to mentees (Burke, Mckenna, & McKenna, 1993; Fagenson-Eland et al., 1997; Johnson-Bailey & Cervero, 2002; Koberg, Boss, & Goodman, 1998; Ragins & McFarlin, 1990). Within the university, mentors can be instructors, counselors, student affairs professionals, and senior peers. In the university, students have plenty of opportunities to develop a good relationship with these professionals. Even their senior peers may provide good support for them. Mentoring can bring long-term benefits (Chao, 1997). In a content analysis, Allen, Poteet, and Burroughs (1997) found that mentees improved their overall academic performance during the school year. According to Scandura (1992), mentors can provide the following to mentees:
- Academic development
- Career development
- Psychosocial functions: role modeling, counseling, and friendship
- Social support

In the ExCEL group session, the group leader begins by asking the students if they have someone to support them who can offer help when they need it. Then, s/he discusses the benefits of mentors and suggests ways of finding a mentor if students do not have one yet. S/he also discusses how to develop a mentoring relationship and how to get the most out of this experience.

EXCEL GROUP
SESSION 7: FIND A MENTOR

Objectives:
1. Students will understand mentoring and its benefits.
2. Students will learn how to find a mentor.

Procedure:
1. What is a mentor? (10 minutes)
   Mentor is a person who provides:
      - nurturing
      - guidance
      - support
2. Why do I need a mentor? (5 minutes)
3. Do you have a mentor or someone who supports you when you need help? (15 minutes)
4. How can I find a mentor here at the University? (45 minutes)
   - Start in your academic department, the faculty/staff you always contact on campus.
   - Look for common interests between you and the prospective mentor.
   - Test the water.
   - Possible mentors: instructor, advisors/counselors, student affairs professionals, family members, friends, community/religious leaders, and student leaders
   - Take time and be realistic.
5. Summary and assignment – 10 minutes
   - What did you learn today? (group reflections)
   - Start to look for a mentor and report your progress to the group in the next meeting.

Session Eight: Living in A Multicultural Society

In the eighth group session, the topic is developing skills for living in a multicultural society. Literature shows that academic performance relates to how well students can handle racism and gender bias on a predominantly Caucasian campus (Bennett, 2002; Nora & Cabrera, 1996; Sedlacek, 1987; Wilds, 2000; Wright, 1987). On the other hand, women also face barriers to their development and achievement (Ancis & Sedlacek, 1997; Fuertes Sedlacek & Liu, 1994; Fuertes & Sedlacek, 1995). The focus in this session is to increase student awareness of racial/ethnic and gender diversity as well as to improve personal skills in dealing with such challenges or stereotypes.

This session is conducted in role-play exercises. In practice, the students found the role play activities very useful in revealing some of their biases and pre-assumptions. Some of the uncensored words expressed by the students were powerful. Therefore, laying down the ground rules for judgment or criticism is essential for the role-playing activities. Also, the students learned some assertiveness skills that they may use in racial/gender confrontations or other biased situations.

EXCEL GROUP
SESSION 8
LIVING IN A MULTICULTURAL SOCIETY

Objectives:
1. Students will understand their positions in the multicultural society.
2. Students will learn about stereotypes against ethnic groups/women.
3. Students will learn in role play how to deal with racial/gender stereotypes.

Procedures:
I. Review of last meeting - 5 minutes

II. First thoughts on an ethnic, racial or gender group - 5 minutes
   a. In the group, leader calls out names of ethnic groups, gender, religion, etc.
   b. Group members immediately say the uncensored thoughts associated with the names.
   c. The leader asks for feedback from the group and processes the comments.

III. Internalized oppression and pride - 15 minutes
   a. Form groups in twos that belong to same ethnic, gender or religious group.
   b. The first person points a finger at the partner and says the negative stereotypes of the group while the second person listens.
   c. Exchange feedback.
   d. First person says things they are proud of concerning their group.
   e. Exchange feedback.
   f. Group leader processes this activity in the larger group

IV. Coaching for behavior change - 40 minutes
   Leader demonstrates how to interrupt bigoted comments. Then, s/he asks the group to practice.
   a. Group members generate a list of bigoted jokes, remarks and slurs most frequently heard on campus.
   b. Students select the most common one from the list.
   c. Role-play the selected joke, remark or slur.
   d. Comments and effects responses (verbal) from the group members.
   e. Practice in groups of twos
   f. Leader process the experience

V. Share a time when racism takes place - 20 minutes
   - Select one/two situations to role-play about how to interrupt effectively the incident.

VI. Summary - Sum up what you learned today - 5 minutes

VII. Assignments: Complete the worksheet: How multicultural is my life?

Session Nine: Getting Involved in Extra-Curricular Activities

In the ninth session the topic is getting involved in extra-curricular activities. Students who become involved in extra-curricular activities and have leadership experiences are found to achieve well in college. Ting (2000) found that successful leadership experiences can explain 5% additional variance for Asian American students' grade-point-average (GPA). Other studies also show that involvement in activities and leadership experiences enhance academic performance (Astin, 1993; Liu & Sedlacek, 1999; Ting, 1997; Ting & Robinson, 1998; Tracey & Sedlacek, 1984; 1985; 1987; 1988; 1989). Assertiveness was found to be a skill useful for nontraditional students (Sedlacek, 2003). In this group session, the objective is to motivate students to get involved in extra-curricular activities on campus and to acquire the skills that benefit their academic development.

In the ExCEL group session, some students talked about how busy they were and how they could not join extra-curricular activities. Others were more active and were involved in some on-campus activities. Ethnic minority students often participated in multicultural student clubs to be connected and to get support. They were encouraged to participate in other activities/student groups. Students who were involved would usually get close to professional advisors or student affairs professionals in student activities, multicultural student services, and special support programs. Ultimately, they may strength their connections to the campus, enhance their social skills, and develop leadership skills. Focused on different challenges, the ExCEL group discusses how students might overcome scheduling issues and become involved in such activities. The group leader follows up to help the students continue to be involved in student activities in the remaining group sessions and individual student meetings.

EXCEL GROUP
SESSION 9
GETTING INVOLVED IN EXTRA-CURRICULAR ACTIVITIES

Objectives:
1. To introduce extra-curricular activities on campus.
2. To motivate students to get involved in extra-curricular activities.
3. To discuss the benefits of being involved in extra-curricular activities.

Preparation:
1. Collect information about extra-curricular activities on campus.
   (Hint: Ask the Student Activities Office for more information.)
2. Read the information and be familiar with some of the activities.

Procedures
1. Review last meeting - 10 minutes

2. Introduce the extra-curricular activities - 15 minutes
3. Ask students about their participation in extra-curricular activities - 20 minutes
   Samples questions:
   What did you do in extra-curricular activities in high school?
   If you were not involved much, why?
   What do you do now in extra-curricular activities on campus?
   If you are not involved in any of these activities, what do you do in your leisure time?
   Could you share about your experiences in extra-curricular activities in this university?
   What positions/roles do you play in these activities?
   Why do you join these activities?
4. Discuss benefits of participation - 30 minutes
   (You may discuss the challenges and struggles as well)
   Provide information that research studies have found that college students who are more involved in extra-curricular activities (or are student leaders) are more likely to be academically successful.
5. Reflections and summary of the group meeting - 15 minutes
   What have the group members learned from this meeting?
   Will this meeting influence their involvement in extra-curricular activities? How?
6. Application: Ask students to join one or two student groups.

Session Ten:
Integration and Evaluation

In the last session, Session 10, the group leader helps the students integrate their whole group process, learning, and experiences. This is also the time for evaluation as well as an ethical requirement by the Association of Small Group Work (read more from Chapter 8 Group Evaluation).

As the group ends, certain tasks need to be achieved (Corey 2003; Yalom & Leszcz, 2005):

- Help the students adjust to the ending of the group.
- Allow time for students to reflect on their experiences.
- Discuss any unfinished business or problems with other group members.
- Discuss what to do to continue to develop in the areas each group topic covered.
- Find out how students may receive continuing support.
- Conduct group evaluation.

It is a good practice to begin the last session by asking the students to summarize what they have learned. Naturally, the leader may move on to unfinished business, for example, personal issues not discussed or topics not covered. It will be beneficial for every group member to share thoughts and comments about other members: compliments, impressions, and words of encouragement.

Group leaders should be prepared to deal with negative feelings that may come up. They should also explore issues of separation. How may the termination of the group affect the students? Some students learn a lot from the ExCEL group and are more ready to continue on their own, and others may need more time and continuing support. In these cases, what kind of support they can get if they need help? Professional support and services can be provided, such as advising centers and counseling services. Also, Yalom and Leszcz (2005) suggested continuing the groups without a leader as an informal support group; the leader may occasionally visit the group as a consultant to help the transition.

Finally, the group leader should conduct some evaluation of the group outcomes, which will be discussed in the next chapter.

Chapter 8:
Group Evaluation

Evaluation is very important in group work, so I adopt different instruments and tools to evaluate group outcomes. The Learning and Study Strategies Inventory is designed to assess student's study skills such as time management, coping with anxiety, concentration, and information process. Grade-point-average (GPA) and student retention are academic indicators taken into account during evaluation. And case study is another valuable approach for evaluating group outcomes, as descriptive data often tells what numbers cannot. In exit interviews, participating ExCEL students meet with the group leader individually to review their experiences and progress in the group. The group leader asks questions developed from the Non-Cognitive Questionnaire about students' psychosocial development, particularly in terms of problem areas identified at the beginning of the process.

The Learning and Study Strategies Inventory (LASSI; Weinstein & Palmer, 1987) is designed to measure students' use of learning strategies and study methods. There are ten scales on the LASSI, including (a) Attitude, (b) Motivation, (c) Time Management, (d) Coping with Anxiety, (e) Concentration, (f) Information Processing, (g) Selecting Main Ideas, (h) Study Aids, (I) Self Testing, and (j) Test Skills. Each scale contains eight items, except for "Selecting Main Ideas," which has five items. The total possible score on the individual scales is 40, except for "Selecting Main Ideas," which is 25. Coefficient alphas for the scales range from .74 to .86, except for "Study Aids," which is .68. Test-rest correlation coefficients for the scales range from .72 to .85, demonstrating a high degree of stability for the scale scores. Olejnik and Nist (1992) propose that the LASSI measures 3 latent variables: effort-related activities (motivation, time management, concentration), goal orientation (anxiety, test strategies, main ideas selection), and cognitive activities (information processing, study aids utilization and self testing). Certainly, other instruments measuring study skills can be adopted to assess the progress of the ExCEL students. However, Olenjnik and Nist (1992) suggest that the LASSI can be used to examine the effectiveness of educational interventions; I maintain that using the LASSI may effectively evaluate the benefits of ExCEL, specifically benefits pertaining to academic success at the university.

Exit Interview

To find out the ExCEL group member's perspectives on their changes, the group leader interviews the members individually after the final group session. Interview is always used as a qualitative approach for research and evaluation (Seidman, 2006). It provides information from the field: A structure for in-depth, phenomenological interviewing. Each ExCEL student is interviewed for about thirty to forty minutes in a semi-structured format with a few open-ended questions:

1. What did you learn from the group sessions?
2. Did you see yourself improve in non-cognitive (psychosocial) areas? If so, which areas?
3. How did the changes happen?
4. What ExCEL group topics did you like the most?
5. What were the strengths of the ExCEL group?
6. What were the areas for improvements for the ExCEL group?
7. Will you recommend the ExCEL group to others?

Case Study

Individual student cases were studied (Berg, 2007); changes in student development, adjustment, and academic success were examined. In the beginning of ExCEL group, characteristics of students were recorded, such as name, age, ethnicity, gender, socio-economic status, and academic background such as class, major, studying problems, and challenges. Next, their non-cognitive variables profiles were studied and discussed. Individual follow-up work included counseling and tutorial services. Formative evaluation, including informal check-ins and feedback, continued throughout the duration of the ExCEL group.

Student case studies allow us to further understand the outcomes of the ExCEL groups. Here are some examples of case studies. All cases are real (with names changed).

Case Study
Phil Fine

Philomena (Phil) Fine is a Caucasian woman in her late 30s. She has served in the army, and once she completes her degree in agricultural science, she needs to return to the army for three additional year's service. Her major is food science.

Phil is married and has two sons aged 16 and 7, who live in another state about 4 hours away. Her husband is a retired soldier. During some weekends, she drives back home to stay with her family, who have not moved to stay with her here because her sons want to stay in school in their home town. This long distance family situation has caused mixed feelings for her. Usually she studies at her apartment off-campus, yet she is not well motivated to study. Neither does she participate in any extra-curricular activities or receive any tutorials from the Academic Support Program on her campus.

Phil is a typical non-traditional student who has returned to college. She has chosen agricultural science not because of her interest, but because the army will pay the tuition for this discipline. She has shown little interest in agricultural science. Having left her family in another state, she always feels lonely and bored at the university. No wonder she has told me that she often watches TV at her apartment off-campus. She needs some good motivation, and her major problem is that she needs to be involved in extra-curricular/community activities to enhance the integration of her college life.

Phil joined the group voluntarily. During the group sessions, she was very attentive and participated in the discussions. At the interview after all group sessions were completed, she told me that she found some improvements in different areas. These included:
1. Increased attention on how to review chapters/lectures notes,
2. Enjoyed the exercises and activities related to participating in co-curricular/community activities,
3. Spent less time on TV now, and
4. Incorporated better self-discipline into her life.

Case Study
John Doe

John is the only man in the group and he is 19. He is an Asian American whose major is Biology. He is second generation Chinese from California whose family is originally from Hong Kong. His father is a motel manager, and his mother is a housekeeper. During weekends, he sometimes stays with his uncle, who lives in a metropolitan area which is 40 miles away from the campus.

John's studying problems relate to his self-concept and personal characteristics. He is not motivated to focus on his studies and likes to skip classes. He always has day dreams and has found it difficult to concentrate while studying. On campus, he has become active by getting involved with the International Student Association, and he enjoys staying with his peers who are students from Hong Kong.

John does not have any goals for the future but seems to like the natural environment. He plans to transfer back to California next year.

John's non-cognitive variable problems are negative self-concept and lack of a long term goal. In social life, he is not comfortable with identifying himself as an American. On the contrary—he relates more with international students from Hong Kong than his American peers. In academics, he seems to be interested in the natural environment; however, he has never thought seriously about choosing this subject as his college major or career. Thus, he is unmotivated in his studies and cannot concentrate in his academic work. Also, he spends very little time (less than an hour per day) on his own studies outside of class.

In the exit interview, he mentioned the following changes that he observed:
1. I can focus on my studies more. But sometimes, I still do day dream.
2. I know more about myself, and I feel good.

3. I think that I learned more about how to study more effectively.
4. I feel like I have a better sense of my personal goals and have started to plan for them.

At the end of the academic year, finally, he decided not to transfer back to California; instead, he has continued to study at his original university and has selected natural resource management as his major.

Follow-Up Evaluation: GPA and Student Retention

Students' grade-point-average (GPA) is a focus of the follow-up evaluation, since GPA provides direct evidence of academic success. In evaluation, GPAs, which could range from 0 to 4.0, were used as an indicator for academic performance. Another indicator of academic progress, student retention, is measured by registration status—that is, remaining enrolled vs. dropping out. Students' GPAs and evidence of continuing enrollment are usually obtained from the university records. For the purposes of evaluation, usually first year semester GPAs were compared between ExCEL and non-ExCEL students; it was expected that ExCEL student GPAs would be better than those of the non-ExCEL students. Student retention was also studied to see if the ExCEL group's retention could be explained by non-cognitive variables.

In addition to the above methods, other evaluation methods and tools including portfolios, journals, essays, and artifacts can also be considered (Sedlacek, 2004).

In the next chapters, research studies on ExCEL groups will be presented, along with detailed information of the research study method and implications of outcomes for practice.

Chapter 9:
Research Studies

Field studies of the ExCEL group model are reported in this chapter. Different student groups were studied, including the academically under-prepared, adult students, low-income, first-generation, students living on campus, ethnic minorities, and freshmen seminars. Each study will be reported in the following format, covering participants, procedures, and results. The discussion at the end of the chapter provides some insights and implications for professional practice.

Research Study Method

The research study method includes the quantitative approach of pre-and-post tests using the Learning and Study Strategies Inventory (LASSI; Weinstein & Palmer, 1987)(See Ch. 8 Group Evaluation) and GPAs and retention rate, and the qualitative approach of individual interviews and case studies. In case studies, I have recorded personal profiles of the students including their non-cognitive problem areas, which are compared at the end of the group meetings.

Students' grade-point-average (GPA) is a common indicator for academic performance and a focus in the research studies. In information collection, GPAs, which could range from 0 to 4.0, were used as an indicator for students' academic performance. Also, student retention is measured by registration status, that is, remaining enrolled (represented by 1) or dropping out (represented by 0). Students' GPAs and continuing enrollment, after receiving consent from the students, are usually obtained from the university records.

Students are usually separated into treatment and control group for evaluation or research study. Typically, background of treatment and control group students are matched using attributes such as age, gender, ethnicity, and academic background (status in progress towards graduation and test scores).

To find out the ExCEL group members' perspectives on changes in college adjustment and academic success, the group leader interviews the members individually after the last group session. The interview follows a semi-structured format with a few open-ended questions.

In the beginning of ExCEL group, the characteristics of students are recorded such as name, age, ethnicity, gender, socio-economic status, and academic background such as class, major, studying problems and challenges. Next, their non-cognitive variables profiles are studied and discussed. Individual follow-up work includes counseling and tutorial services. Formative evaluation continues until the end of the ExCEL group.

Research Questions

The EXCEL group aims to enhance students' academic performance and psychosocial development. Typically, I ask the following questions in research

studies, after completion of group sessions:
1. Did the students in the treatment group improve their LASSI scores?
2. Did the students in the treatment group improve in non-cognitive areas?
3. Did the students in the treatment group exhibit a higher GPA than did those in the control group?
4. Did the students in the treatment group show a higher retention rate than did those in the control group?

Wisconsin Group

The first ExCEL group was created in the University of Wisconsin-River Falls in 1994 (Ting, 1997b). I conducted an extensive recruitment effort; all freshmen who registered in the academic support TRIO program or minority student services were invited to join the group. Finally, eleven freshmen enrolled in the ExCEL group, including 9 females and 2 males and all but two completed the group sessions. Five students of the group were Asian Americans, which reflected the fact that the largest minority group on campus was Asian and the rest were Caucasians. The mean age was 22.3 ($n = 9$) reflecting the four of the group members who were adult students.

Treatment and Control Group

The ExCEL group (n = 10), or the treatment group, was compared to a control group who were students ($n = 173$) in the TRIO program but did not participate in the group. GPA and retention were compared between the treatment group and the control group.

Results

First, the results showed that group members' scale scores on the Learning and Study Strategies Inventory (Weinstein & Palmer, 1987) improved. All scales scores showed mean gains of over 1.0. The largest mean gains were found in: Coping with Anxiety (+2.8), Concentration (+4), Information Processing (+4.4), Selecting Main Ideas (+3.1) and Test Skills (+2.9).

Research question two was analyzed by student interview. At the end of the group process, the students reported increased knowledge about self, better self-appraisal systems, more skills in coping with anxiety, improved time-management, reduced feeling of pressure about academics, enriched knowledge outside of textbooks and classes, and earlier planning for future careers. During the interview, all students expressed satisfaction with the group and said they would recommend the group to other students.

For research question three, it was found that the ExCEL group members' mean GPAs (2.8) were higher than those of other freshmen in the TRIO program (2.3; $n = 173$). In terms of the final research question, the ExCEL group members' retention rate was 89%, significantly higher than were other freshmen in the TRIO program (70%; $n = 173$).

In summary, the results of the first ExCEL group in Wisconsin provided preliminary evidence of the effectiveness of the non-cognitive group intervention.

Residence Halls

The ExCEL group was repeated at another campus, North Carolina State University (NC State). Twelve resident students, recruited by mail and in classes, began the ExCEL program in 1996 (Ting, Grant, & Plenert, 2000).

Treatment and Control Group

For the sake of research, the NC State group and the Wisconsin group were combined for data analysis, giving a data sample of 22 participants, 17 of them completed the group. Control groups ($n = 26$) were selected from students through Student Support Services ($n=184$) for sub-sample I, the Wisconsin group and student records ($N = 2849$) for sub-sample II, the NC State undergraduate students. Gender, race, previous grades/class ranks, and standardized test scores (either the American College Test (ACT) or Scholastic Aptitude Test (SAT)) of the treatment and control groups were matched. For sub-sample I, the mean high school percentile ranks of the ExCEL students and the control group were 36.89 and 33.56, respectively, and mean ACT composite scores were 18.44 and 18.39, respectively. Mean high school GPAs were 3.28 and 3.28, respectively, and mean SAT total scores were 999 and 1025, respectively for treatment and control groups of sub-sample II. There were 19 females and three males in the treatment group and 21 females and five males in the control group. The treatment group consisted of nine Caucasians, three African-Americans, and five Asian-Americans, while the control group was made up of 20 Caucasians, three African-Americans, and three Asian-Americans.

Data Analysis

Ranking of the difference between pretest-and-posttest LASSI scores for members of the treatment group across all sub-samples were analyzed using nonparametric inferential tests due to the small number of students (less than 30) in the study. GPA and student enrollment of treatment participants was compared with those of the control groups using the Wilcoxon Signed Ranks Test for sub-sample I and the Mann-Whitney Test for sub-sample II. Common themes were drawn from interview data.

Results

In sub-sample I, significant differences were found on the Learning and Study Strategies Inventory (LASSI) subscales of Concentration ($Z = -2.31, p < .02$), Information Processing ($Z = 2.43, p < .02$), Selecting Main Ideas ($Z = -2.49, p <$

.01), and Test Skills ($Z = -2.32$, $p < .02$). These results indicate that after the program was completed, the students performed better in these areas. Similar results were found for sub-sample II. Also, the ExCEL participants performed better on the subscales of Coping with Anxiety ($Z = -2.21$, $p < .03$), Information Processing ($Z = -2.38$, $p < .02$), Selecting Main Ideas ($Z = -2.38$, $p < .02$), and Self Testing ($Z = -2.36$, $p < .02$).

For sub-sample I, employing Mann-Whitney Test, significant differences of first semester GPAs between ExCEL and non-ExCEL students were found ($M = 2.65$, $SD = .23$ vs. $M = 2.05$, $SD = .66$; mean ranks = 20.39 and 10.81 for treatment and control groups respectively; $U = 23.5$, $Z = -2.96$, $p < .003$). The treatment group performed better in GPA at the completion of the groups. A Wilcoxon Signed Ranks Test was computed for sub-sample II, and similar results were found ($M = 2.96$, $SD = .64$ vs. $M = 2.26$, $SD = .88$ for treatment and control groups respectively; mean negative rank = 0 and mean positive rank = 45; $Z = -2.51$, $p < .01$). Significant differences were found in the rank differences between the GPA of the treatment and control groups; treatment group GPAs were higher.

Student retention is another aspect always considering when studying programs that strive to affect student success. In this study, the retention rate for the first sub-sample (89%) after the first year was higher than that of the control group (83%). However, when comparing the ranking of enrollment status by the Mann-Whitney Test, no significant differences were found between the treatment and control groups (mean rank = 14.5 and 13.75 respectively; $U = 76.5$, $Z = -.37$, $p = .71$). Employing the Wilcoxon test for sub-sample II, no significant differences were found in the signed ranks difference of enrollment status (mean negative rank = 0, mean positive rank = 1; $Z = -1.0$, $p = .32$).

I examined students' noncognitive/psychosocial changes through individual interview. Enhanced psychosocial development was reported by the EXCEL students, for example: increased knowledge about themselves, better self-appraisal systems, more skills in coping with anxiety, improved time-management skills, decreased feelings of academic pressure, enriched knowledge from textbooks and classes, and enhanced planning for future careers.

University Transition Program

In the third round, the ExCEL group was expanded by working with a freshman seminar at NC State in 1997 (Ting, 1999). ECD 101 is a one-credit course which is required for all students enrolled in the University Transition Program (UTP). The program admits students who are academically under-prepared, with lower high school GPA and SAT scores. Most of the students in the program belong to ethnic minorities or are students from non-traditional backgrounds. The course is designed to enhance students' academic performance and develop an enriched campus life through related group activities. See Appendix Four for a syllabus of the ECD 101 Orientation to College.

Treatment and Control Group

The seminar had already been offered to students for about 6 years before the ExCEL group intervention was adopted. In 1997, it was re-organized based on the ExCEL model. Fifty-six students of the four sections of first year seminar were invited to participate in the study as treatment groups. Each class had about 14 students. There were 38 males and 18 females. In terms of ethnicity, 41 were African Americans, 11 were Caucasians, 3 were Hispanics, and 1 was an Asian American. A control group ($n = 26$) made up of students with similar high school GPAs, SAT scores, ethnicity, age, and gender was obtained through university records.

Results

A few t-tests were computed to examine if the pretest-and-posttest mean scores of the Learning and Study Strategies Inventory were different. The UTP student posttest mean scores on time management, concentration, information processing, selecting main ideas, use of support techniques and test taking were found to be significantly higher than those of the pretest scores. Also, the fall GPAs of the treatment and control group were compared. In results, the students in the UTP seem to have a higher mean fall GPA than the control group students (2.30 vs. 1.91).

To compare the student retention at the end of the freshman year between the UTP students and the control group, a chi-square test was conducted. It was found that the retention ratio of the UTP group (92.8%) was significantly different from that of the control group (76.9%) ($X^2 = 4.21$, $df = 1$; $p = .04$). The UTP students had a higher retention rate than that of the control group.

The UTP instructors also evaluated students' noncognitive changes through individual interviews. The students reported enhanced psychosocial development such as increased self-confidence, more skills in coping with anxiety, better self-appraisal systems, new knowledge in how to study in a field, and development of academic major or longer-term goals.

Based on the findings, since 1997, the UTP continues to include the non-cognitive approach and topics in their classes every year with about 60 to 70 students and has benefited many students from non-traditional backgrounds.

Retention Program at First Year College

Another group program with the objective of student retention was implemented based on the ExCEL model at NC State in 1998 (Stonehouse & Ting, 2000). All participants were recruited from a population of students at the First Year College who had been placed on academic warning at the end of the first semester. The students' GPA was between 1.5 and 1.9, and they were considered academically at risk of dropping out; need for academic intervention was clear.

Treatment and Control Group

These students were invited to join the program through mailing. The treatment group, therefore, were students who enrolled in the program ($n = 28$). Of this group, 4(14%) were female and 24 (86%) were male. The participants were classified as Caucasian (78%), African American (14%), and Asian American (7%). Ages ranged from 18 to 20.

A matched control group of 28 students was selected from the list of all first-year students placed on academic warning at the end of the fall 1997. Students were matched based on their fall semester GPA, gender, and race.

The program formulated for this study, Renewed Commitment Program (RCP; Stonehouse & Ting, 2000) was developed based on the ExCEL model and other interventions. The program consists of:

1. Reflections groups
   These groups provided an opportunity for students to discuss common challenges (such as topics in the ExCEL group including study skills, self-esteem, etc.) and reflect on possible enhancements through discussion with peers in the group. The group met once per week for an hour and a half.
2. Individual meetings
   Group leaders conducted one-on-one meetings with the students to allow more time for personal attention and support. At these meetings, personal issues and concerns were explored in more depth and a personalized plan of success was collaboratively developed.
3. Success lab
   The Success Lab was designed for students to practice the skills or strategies they learned in the other two components. Students visited the lab for at least one hour per week, and they developed a short-term goal for improving their studies during the scheduled time. Professional counselors and tutors were available to assist students in meeting those goals.

Results

The results show that the RCP group earned an average Spring semester GPA of 1.989 while the control group students earned only 1.815. However, the t-test show that the RCP students did not have a higher mean spring GPA ($t_{27} = -1.02$, $p < .38$) than the control group. As for the retention rate, more of the RCP students enrolled for spring 1998 than the control group students ($t_{27} = 2.16$, $p < .04$).

Discussion

The overall results of the research studies appear to be positive; such interventions enhance students' academic performance and their noncognitive/psychosocial development. First, the improved LASSI post-test scores of the ExCEL group may reflect the effectiveness of the group process which covered topics corresponding to these LASSI scales. In the first study in Wisconsin, improvements occurred in understanding of a multicultural society, involvement in extra-curricular activities, knowledge about self, awareness of self-appraisal systems, enhanced concentration in studying, and reduced level of anxiety. Sedlacek (1991) also reported similar results that individuals improved in self-concept and self-appraisal systems by attending one-on-one advising. For other non-cognitive variables in which no improvements were exhibited, students at least reported increased awareness or initiated attempts to make progress were recorded, such as attempts to read more than textbooks (knowledge in a field), looking for a strong support person and planning for a career. Such improvements or increased awareness may have helped to improve the ExCEL students' GPAs and retention rate.

In light of discussing personal adjustment issues and developmental concerns, the small group size in the current study appeared to be ideal. However, the fact that ExCEL participants were all volunteers, and as a consequence highly motivated to make improvements in study skills and psychosocial development, could bias the results. Also, some earlier studies had a small group size at Wisconsin and the residence group at NC State. However, the ExCEL group was later adopted and expanded into a comparatively large first-year seminar, the University Transition Program. This specific study confirms the earlier findings on improvements of academic performance, student retention, and psychosocial development.

Recent studies show that learning experiences in extra-curricular activities were found to be important to students' successful academic and social adjustment (Kuh et al., 1991). In particular, academically high-risk students who had leadership experiences and participation in community services were more likely to be successful in college (Hood, 1992; Ting, 1998; White & Sedlacek, 1986). In addition, other psychosocial variables, such as current level of and importance of personal development, sensitivity to diversity, and communication skills were found to be related to student success in the first year (Ting & Robinson, 1998). Therefore, intervention programs designed to enhance the academic performance of college freshmen may benefit from new strategies derived from recent studies.

To conclude: using the ExCEL model of academic success in the empirical studies, I examined the model's effectiveness. The results of the studies imply that counselors and advisors use of such a non-cognitive model can effectively improve academic performance and retention for the students enrolled in academic support programs like TRIO, freshmen seminar, and residency programs. Many of the students in the ExCEL group were non-traditional students. Therefore, counselors and student service professionals working with non-traditional students may consider this approach. Furthermore, using a small group approach may be one of the keys explaining the success of this intervention model. Small groups with guided focus on community building provide students with an informal, interactive and supportive environment. The approach appears to have worked well with students who were adults, academically underprepared or ethnic minorities. To increase the effectiveness of retention programs, counselors and student affairs professionals need to help improve the cognitive and non-cognitive domains of these students.

A limitation is that most of the group size was comparatively small. However, the repeated studies show consistent findings, which increase the credibility of the effectiveness of the ExCEL model.

Chapter 10:
What's next?

The ExCEL program is a support group specially designed for non-traditional students. Reviewing the past chapters, a list of successful elements is proposed for discussion. To develop a successful group intervention program for college students, counseling and student service professionals may consider these elements.

Successful Elements for the ExCEL Group

To develop the ExCEL or other similar groups, one must have a good knowledge of the environment and the challenges of all students on a given campus. These problems vary from campus to campus, depending on a number of factors such as institution history, geographic location, institutional nature, mission, size, and multicultural climate. Understanding the factors that combine to make up each campus' set of unique challenges is essential and fundamental for designing the group in terms of goals and activities.

In addition to the Non-Cognitive Questionnaire (Sedlacek, 2004), there are other instruments that are useful for appraising non-traditional student populations. For example, the Situational Attitude Scale (Sedlacek, 1996) is an instrument designed to identify non-traditional students who face challenges, bias and discrimination because of their background. Other models focus on eliminating racism, such as Helms' model (1995) and that of Sedlacek and Brooks (1976). Whatever instruments professionals may choose, they are encouraged to study the local situations and understand the challenges of students on their campuses. This is important for designing an intervention intended to improve students' abilities to cope with the difficulties imposed by the environment.

Next, it will be critical to have intentional program objectives. Like many other student programs, clearly and specifically stated objectives will set the right path for the program and help attract the target groups of students. Intentional interventions are not new to college student services. In their Practice-to-Theory-to Practice model, Wells and Knefelkamp (1984) proposed that all student programs should be intentional and designed with specific goals from the beginning. Winston, Bonney, Miller, & Dangley (1988) concurred, and added that the common objectives shared by all group members should be discussed well in the group.

Intentional program objectives will help target and attract non-traditional students for recruitment. Also, in order to recruit students successfully, outcomes from previous group work should be publicized, as these early successes will increase students' confidence about the groups. Having high level administrators support the program by attending the information meeting for recruiting students—as they may for many school programs, such as academic and sports organizations—may also send a powerful message to students.

College is a community; collaboration is highly promoted by student services and, indeed, almost all programs in higher education. Collaborating with academic departments or programs and giving academic credits to students for attending a class will help create more incentives for students and can develop an on-going structure for the ExCEL group. Institutional support, which provides the human and financial resources, structure, and facilities for first-year program, is essential. For example, since the ExCEL model was adopted by the University Transition Program (UTP) at North Carolina State University, every year, about 70 to 80 academically high risk students enroll in the UTP. Connecting to academic programs also builds collaboration between the ExCEL group and faculty/instructors. For example, counseling and student service internships have been developed benefiting both first-year UTP students and graduate interns. In student services, involving professionals such as those working in multicultural services would be natural for non-traditional students. During recruiting for the initial ExCEL program, about 200 students received information through the support and networking between the Academic Support Office and the Multicultural Student Services at the University of Wisconsin-River Falls. Starting a group is not easy, particularly on a small campus; however, the first ExCEL group was established and completed successfully through collaborative efforts.

In the ExCEL group, many sessions on non-cognitive topics are conducted from a cognitive-behavioral approach founded on challenge and support. Students are exposed to information or intellectual processes which challenge their situations. For example, they are asked to review their self-appraisal skills and practice improving their academic performance. Meanwhile, support through the group process and the group leader is given to promote change/improvement.

Involving peer group leaders in group design always provides new perspectives and creative ideas for the ExCEL group. They may be graduate counseling students or counseling interns who are prepared to lead small groups. At North Carolina State University, two ExCEL groups were implemented in student residence halls. They were led by counseling interns, who were also the hall directors for these residence halls.

The group members themselves must also provide input for group design; as the group begins, the group leader needs to be flexible in the group sessions. At times, students may desire to spend more time on a particular topic. For example, one ExCEL group showed more interest in learning study skills for college classes, while another ExCEL group was more inclined to the topics related to self-appraisal and developing long term goals. Therefore, group leaders for ExCEL need to ask the group about collective and individual interests in the beginning of the group process and should be prepared to adjust the topics for each session.

Finally, assessment is an important part of the ExCEL group process. Specific and detailed plans for assessment reflecting the group objectives are vital for evaluating the outcomes (Upcraft, 2005). Charting a good research design for group intervention is essential. Pre-and-post-test design allows an objective comparison of the academic performance of the students before and after intervention. Setting up a control group with backgrounds and experiences similar to those of the test group will provide a good comparison with the ExCEL (treatment) group and help eliminate the bias created by the voluntary nature of group attendance.

Gardner, Upcraft, and Barefoot (2005) also suggested principles of good practice for the first college year, which include:
- Institutional support
- A focus on student learning
- Partnerships between academic affairs and student affairs
- A balance between challenge and support
- High standards of academic performance and personal conduct
- Inclusive campus climate and supportive environment
- Systematic assessment
- Teaching students the strategies and skills for success
- Faculty Involvement
- Students assuming responsibility for their own success

Based on their national study of college first-year programs, Gardner, Upcraft, and Barefoot's (2005) proposed principles are reasonable, practical and necessary for the success of first-year programs. When we compare the list of successful elements with principles of good practice for the first college year, there are similarities. Both of the two lists focus on institutional support and partnerships (or collaboration) between academic affairs and student affairs. Also, they emphasize teaching students study skills and other strategies for a successful academic experience in higher education. The ExCEL group, stresses acquiring both cognitive and non-cognitive skills. Academics are a part of the mix; cognitive topics such as learning and study skills are emphasized and always put in the beginning sessions of the ExCEL group. Good assessment to provide credible information about the program outcomes and effectiveness is necessary as well.

Looking Into the Future

In addition to teaching and counseling, higher education institutions have adopted non-cognitive variables (NCVs) for use in admissions, financial aid, support programs and evaluation. Some successes were found and more of similar kinds of work or activities should be pursued and critically examined.

Admissions

At NC State University, the non-cognitive variables were studied to examine their predictability for academic success (Hill, 1995; Ting & Robinson, 1998, Ting & Sedlacek, 2000). In the results, self-concept and long-term goals were the best predictor of college GPA for Caucasian applicants, while self-concept and ability to live in a multicultural community were the best predictors of their retention. Self-concept, access to a strong support person, and handling racism were the best predictors of college grades and retention for students of color. In another study at NC State University, Hoey (1997) reported that college first-year fall GPA and NCQ scores predicted accurately 92 percent of the retention of African American students advancing from the first year to the second year. Similar factors were found predicting correctly 92 percent for their retention from the first year to the second year for students of color. Based on the outcomes, NC State has incorporated the NCQ variables into their application form and has used them along with other cognitive variables such as SAT scores for admissions.

Oregon State University has used the NCVs for admissions for six years, and the Latino student enrollment has gone up from 432 to 775 in that six year period. In the Insight Resume required by the admissions package, applicants responded to six NCV questions. The real evidence for the success of the new admissions criteria is in academic performance: higher scores on the Insight Resume were related to retention rates. Average GPAs also increased slightly (Sedlacek, 2004).

Other universities also adopted the NCVs for admissions. For example, an eastern private liberal arts college increased their applicant pool by 18 percent over three years after adopting the NCVs for admissions. Self concept and long-term goals correlated highest with success at the college. A large Southern state university applied the NCQ to nontraditional applicants and NCVs were weighted about 60%, compared to 40% for the ACT scores and high school grades (Sedlacek, 2004). The university also trained their admissions staff to determine how "traditional" the experience of each applicant was. As a result of employing the NCVs, the university admitted 64% of the African American applicants. The six-year graduation rate after introducing the NCVs was increased from 30% for African American students to 56%. The same graduation rate changed from 60% to 65% for traditional students.

Scholarships and Financial Aid

In addition to applications for admission, NCVs have also been adopted for scholarships and financial aid. The Gates Millennium Scholars program aims to provide financial support for students of color in mathematics, science and technology, education or library science. The selection criteria include leadership ability, community service, and extracurricular activities. The Non-Cognitive Questionnaire (NCQ) was adopted to assess the students along with an evaluation of students' high school course work and an essay.

The Washington State Achievers program began in 2002 to serve the students from lower-income backgrounds who are admitted to Washington state universities. The program staff was trained to identify noncognitive variables and score them along with other information for awards (Sedlacek, 2004).

Other programs that have adopted the NCQ for assessment include the National Action Council for Minorities in Engineering (NACME) and financial aid offices from a number of state universities in different regions in the U.S.

Support Programs and Evaluation

The Department of Mathematics at the University of Maryland adopted noncognitive variables into their questionnaire for new doctoral students. Based on the responses, follow-up programs and services were arranged. These supporting activities include mentoring, peer support (such as study groups), information about community opportunities, sponsorship of student-faculty gatherings, and minority role models. As a result, the retention rate was greatly enhanced, to above 50%, for African American students (Cooper, 1999).

Need for Research

More research on noncognitive strategies for groups in higher education is needed at diverse campuses with greater numbers and different circumstances in order to generalize results, expand benefits, and perfect program design. A larger number of students can be recruited by adopting the ExCEL strategies into first-year seminars. More research is also needed on group process and outcomes of diverse students from non-traditional backgrounds in areas that are not covered here, such as disabilities, sexual orientation, and differences among racial groups. Moreover, all of the ExCEL groups featured here were conducted with undergraduate students. ExCEL group's effect on graduate students can be studied.

Another area for new research is studying new strategies for intervention approach. For example, Goldberg (2001) found that emotional intelligence is related to performance in military personnel; however, few studies can be found in the field of education, particularly on academic performance and success. Motivation is a non-cognitive variable (Ting & Sedlacek, 2000). Involving faculty is proven to be important for college students' performance and motivation (Astin, 1997; Kuh, 1993), but other strategies can be derived from the five basic personality elements that are believed to exist in all people (Goldberg, 2001):

1. Extraversion
2. Agreeableness
3. Conscientiousness
4. Emotional stability
5. Intellect and imagination

Some earlier studies show evidence of success in the balance of these five elements. However, few interventions, including group work, were conducted to assess the effect of emotional intelligence on college students' academic success.

Appendix One:
Non-Cognitive Questionnaire
Adapted from Tracey & Sedlaek (1984)

Please fill in the blank or circle the appropriate answers.

1. Your social security number:_____

2. Your sex is: _____ 1. Male 2. Female

3. Your age is: ___ years

4. Your father's occupation: _____

5. Your mother's occupation: _____

6. Your race is: _____
    1. Black (African-American)
    2. White (not of Hispanic origin)
    3. Asian (Pacific Islander)
    4. Hispanic (Latin American)
    5. American Indian (Alaskan native)
    6. Other

7. How much education do you expect to get during your lifetime?
    1. College, but less than a bachelor's degree
    2. B.A. or equivalent
    3. 1 or 2 years of graduate or professional study (Master's degree)
    4. Doctoral degree such as M.D., Ph.D., etc.

8. Please list three goals that you have for yourself right now:

    1._____
    2._____
    3._____

9. About 50% of university students typically leave before receiving a degree. If this should happen to you, what would be the most likely cause?
    1. Absolutely certain that I will obtain a degree
    2. To accept a good job
    3. To enter military service

4. It would cost more than my family could afford
5. Marriage
6. Disinterest in study
7. Lack of academic ability
8. Insufficient reading or study skills
9. Other

10. Please list three things that you are proud of having done:
    1. _____
    2. _____
    3. _____

Please indicate the extent to which you agree or disagree with each of the following items. Respond to the statements below with your feelings at present or with your expectations of how things will be. Write in your answer to the left of each item.

1	2	3	4	5
Strongly Agree	Agree	Neutral	Disagree	Strongly Disagree

11. The University should use its influence to improve social conditions in the State.
12. It should not be very hard to get a B (3.0) average at UMCP.
13. I get easily discouraged when I try to do something and it doesn't work.
14. I am sometimes looked up to by others.
15. If I run into problems concerning school, I have someone who would listen to me and help me.
16. There is no use in doing things for people, you only find that you get it in the neck in the long run.
17. In groups where I am comfortable, I am often looked to as leader.
18. I expect to have a harder time than most students at UMCP.
19. Once I start something, I finish it.
20. When I believe strongly in something, I act on it.
21. I am as skilled academically as the average applicant to UMCP.
22. I expect I will encounter racism at UMCP.
23. People can pretty easily change me even though I thought my mind was already made up on the subject.
24. My friends and relatives don't feel I should go to college.
25. My family has always wanted me to go to college.
26. If course tutoring is made available on campus at no cost, I would attend regularly.
27. I want a chance to prove myself academically.
28. My high school grades don't really reflect what I can do.
29. Please list offices held and/or groups belonged to in high school or in your community.

Scoring Key for Noncognitive Questionnaire
by William E. Sedlacek (1984)

Questionnaire Item	Variable name (Number)
7	Use to score for Self-Concept (I) Option 1 = 1; 2 = 2; 3 = 3; 4 = 4; No response = 2
8	A. *Options for Long Range Goals* (IV) Each goal is coded according to this scheme: 1 = a vague and/or immediate, short-term goal (e.g., "to meet people," "to get a good schedule," "to gain self confidence") 2 = a specific goal with a stated future orientation which could be accomplished during undergraduate study (e.g., "to join a sorority so I can meet more people," "to get a good schedule so I can get good grades in the fall," "to run for a student government office") 3 = a specific goal with a stated future orientation which would occur after undergraduate study (e.g., "to get a good schedule so I can get the classes I need for graduate school;" "to become president of a Fortune 500 company") B. *Options for Knowledge Acquired in a Field* (VIII) Each goal is coded according to this scheme: 1 = not at all academically or school related; vague or unclear (e.g., "to get married," "to do better," "to become a better person") 2 = school related, but not necessarily or primarily educationally oriented (e.g., "to join a fraternity," "to become student body President") 3 = directly related to education (e.g., "to get a 3.5 GPA," "to get to know my teachers") Find the mean for each dimension (e.g. Long Range Goals) and round to the nearest whole number.

Appendix One

Questionnaire Item	Variable name (Number)
9	Use to score for Self-Concept (I) and Self-Appraisal (II) Option 1 = 4; 2 through 9 = 2; No response = 2
10	Use to score for Self Concept (I) Each accomplishment is coded according to this scheme: 1 = at least 75% of applicants to your school could have accomplished it (e.g., "graduated from high school," "held a part-time summer job") 2 = at least 50% of applicants to your school could have accomplished it (e.g., "played on an intramural sports team," "was a member of a school club") 3 = only top 25% of applicants to your school could have accomplished it (e.g., "won an academic award," "as captain of football team") Find the mean code for this dimension and round to the nearest whole number.

For items 11 through 28, positive (+) items are scored as is. Negative (-) items are reversed, so that 1 = 5, 2 = 4, 3 = 3, 4 = 2, and 5 = 1. A shortcut is to subtract all negative item responses from 6.

Questionnaire Items	Direction	Variable Name (Number)
11	-	Use to score for Racism (III)
12	-	Use to score for Realistic Self-Appraisal (II)
13	+	Use to score for Long-Range Goals (IV)
14	-	Use to score for Leadership (VI)
15	-	Use to score for Availability of Strong Support (V)
16	+	Use to score for Community Service (VII)
17	-	Use to score for Leadership (VI)
18	+	Use to score for Racism (III)
19	-	Use to score for Long-Range Goals (IV)
20	-	Use to score for Positive Self-Concept (I)
21	-	Use to score for Realistic Self-Appraisal (II)
22	-	Use to score for Racism (III)
23	+	Use to score for Positive Self Concept (I)

Appendix One

Questionnaire Items	Direction	Variable Name (Number)
24	+	Use to score for Availability of Strong Support (V)
25	-	Use to score for Availability of Strong Support (V)
26	-	Use to score for Racism (III)
27	-	Use to score for Racism (III)
28	-	Use to score for Positive Self Concept (I)
29		Use to score for Leadership (VI), Community Service (VII) and Knowledge Acquired in a Field (VIII). Each organization is given a code for A, B, and C below. Find the mean for each dimension (e.g. Leadership) and round to the nearest whole number.

A. Leadership (VI)

1 = ambiguous group or no clear reference to activity performed (e.g., "helped in school")

2 = indicates membership but no formal or implied leadership role; it has to be clear that it's a functioning group and, unless the criteria are met for a score of "3" as described below, all groups should be coded as "2" even if you, as the rater, are not familiar with the group (e.g., "Fashionettes," "was part of a group that worked on community service projects through my church")

3 = leadership was required to fulfill role in group (e.g., officer or implied initiator, organizer, or founder) or entrance into the group was dependent upon prior leadership (e.g., "organized a tutoring group for underprivileged children in my community," "student council")

B. Community Service Relatedness (VII)

1 = no community service performed by group, or vague or unclear in relation to community service (e.g., sports team).

2 = some community service involved but it is not the primary purpose of the group (e.g., "Scouts")

3 = group's main purpose is community service (e.g., "Big Brothers/Big Sisters")

C. Knowledge Acquired in a Field (VIII) (same coding criteria as used for item 8B.)

Noncognitive Questionnaire

Worksheet for Scoring

1. POSITIVE SELF-CONCEPT OR CONFIDENCE

    item7* + item9* + item10* + (6 - item20) + item23 + (6 - item28)

2. REALISTIC SELF-APPRAISAL
    item9* + (6 - item12) + (6 - item21)

3. UNDERSTANDS and DEALS with RACISM
    (6 - item11) + item18 + (6 - item22) + (6 - item26) + (6 - item27)

4. PREFERS LONG-RANGE GOALS to SHORT-TERM or IMMEDIATE NEEDS
    item8A* + item13 + (6 - item19)

5. AVAILABILITY of A STRONG SUPPORT PERSON
    (6 - item15) + item24 + (6 - item25)

6. SUCCESSFUL LEADERSHIP EXPERIENCE
    (6 - item14) + (6 - item17) + item29A*

7. DEMONSTRATED COMMUNITY SERVICE
    item16 + item29B*

8. KNOWLEDGE ACQUIRED in a FIELD
    item8B* + item29C*

* Recoded item. See scoring instructions for these items above.

Appendix Two:
Non-Cognitive Questionnaire Revised –2
Siu-Man Raymond Ting and William E. Sedlacek (2000)

Read the following statements and decide if they describe your feelings at present or with your expectation of how things will be. Indicate the extent to which you agree or disagree with each of them. There are no right or wrong answers to the items.

A	B	C	D	E
Strongly Agree	Agree	Neutral	Disagree	Strongly Disagree

1. My high school grades don't really reflect what I can do.
2. I know the areas where I am weak and I try to improve them.
3. My friends and relatives do not feel that I should go to college.
4. I am sometimes looked up to by others.
5. I prefer to be spontaneous rather than to make plans.
6. I expect to be involved in many off-campus community activities while enrolled here.
7. I expect to have little contact with students from other races.
8. I have studied things about my major on my own.
9. I can find a role model from my race to support me.
10. I enjoyed most of my classes in high school.
11. I studied things in high school that enhanced my college study.
12. I prefer to cram for a test than to study for it long before the test.
13. I usually study in a library or a regular place.
14. I can manage my own emotions well.
15. I expect to have a harder time than most students here.
16. I want a chance to prove myself academically.
17. My family always wanted me go to college.
18. In groups where I am comfortable, I am often looked to as a leader.
19. I usually mark important dates on my calendar.
20. I don't expect to get to know faculty personally during my first year.
21. I am comfortable interacting with people from other races or cultures.
22. My friends are exclusively the same race as I am.
23. I have talked about my career goal with someone who works in that career.
24. Most classes in my high school have little practical meaning.
25. I took as many courses as I could in high school to prepare myself for college.
26. I like to converse with faculty out of class.
27. I feel that I am not well prepared academically for college.

28. I can think clearly and maintain focused under pressure.
29. Among my friends, I am popular for understanding other's feelings.
30. It should not be very hard to get a B average here.
31. If tutoring is made available on campus at no cost, I will attend regularly.
32. If I run into problems concerning school, I have someone who would listen to me and help me.
33. I was a student leader in my high school.
34. I know what I want to be doing 10 years from now.
35. I often make lists of things to do.
36. I expect the faculty to treat me differently from the average student here.
37. I enjoy working with others.
38. My background should help me fit in well here.
39. I know my teachers personally in high school.
40. I like to study a variety of subjects.
41. I have a specific goal to attend college.
42. I took more than required courses in high school to prepare for college.
43. I tend to skip classes because they are boring or when I am not in a good mood.
44. Interacting with faculty out of class will benefit my personal growth and development.
45. I cannot concentrate when I am studying.
46. I can motivate myself to achieve a task even when I am emotionally distressed.
47. I stay positive when the situation is unfavorable/hostile.
48. I am as skilled academically as the average applicant of this university.
49. When I believe strongly on something, I act on it.
50. My friends look to me to make decisions.
51. I have already learned something in my proposed major/major outside of high school.
52. I keep to myself pretty much.
53. I am not good at getting others to go along with me.
54. I have (a) role model(s) at home who has/have entered college before me.
55. I prefer to go out to work now than to study in college.
56. I took vigorous and demanding courses in high school.
57. I tend to study only the interesting part in my courses.
58. Interacting with faculty out of class will benefit my career planning and development.
59. I have confidence to get good grades here.
60. I feel comfortable when I am a minority among other races in a social situation.
61. I participated in many extra-curricular activities in high school.
62. I feel discouraged about my academic performance in high school.
63. I am not sure about my career choice.
64. I like to make friends with people of other races.
65. I believe that my studying method is effective.
66. I am empathic with a diversity of people.

Appendix Two

67. I am always aware of my own feelings.
68. I try to find opportunities to learn new things.
69. I find I get more comfortable in a new place as soon as I make good friends.
70. My current goals are related to academics.
71. I can find someone to support me when I need it.

72. How many hours did you spend per week on community service in senior year of high school?
    A. 0   B. 1-5   C. 6-10   D. 11-15   E. 16 and over

73. How many hours did you spend per week in extra-curricular activities in senior year of high school?
    A. 0   B. 1-5   C. 6-10   D. 11-15   E. 16 and over

74. In the first year of college, I plan to work PT or FT job (per week)
    A. 0 hours   B. 1-10 hours   C. 11-20 hours   D. 21-30 hours   E. >30 hours

75. What is your father/male guardian educational level?
    A. high school to high school graduates
    B. some college/ 2-year associate degree
    C. 4-year college degree
    D. master's degree
    E. doctoral degrees

76. What is your mother/female guardian educational level?
    A. high school to high school graduates
    B. some college/ 2-year associate degree
    C. 4-year college degree
    D. master's degree
    E. doctoral degrees

77. How many credits will you take/are you taking in the first semester at this university?
    A. 9 credits or fewer   D. 16 to 18 credits
    B. 10- 12 credits   E. 19 to 21 credits or more
    C. 13 to 15 credits

78. How much education do you expect to get during your lifetime?
    A. College, but less than a bachelor's degree
    B. B.A. or equivalent
    C. 1 or 2 years of graduate or professional study (master's degree)
    D. Doctoral Degree

Scoring Key for Noncognitive Questionnaire-Revised 2 Scales

<u>Instructions:</u>
Add the items for each scale to create scale scores.

1. Academic Self Concept 7 items: 1, 15*, 30, 48, 27*, 59, 62*
2. A Positive Self-appraisal System 5 items: 2, 16, 31, 49, 68
3. Living in a Multicultural Society 7 items: 7*, 22*, 38*, 30, 60, 64, 66
4. A Strong Support Person 6 items: 3*, 17, 32, 71, 9, 54
5. Leadership Experiences 7 items: 4, 18, 33, 50, 53*, 61, 73
6. Long Range Goals 8 items: 5*, 8, 19, 34, 35, 23, 63*, 78*
7. Activities and service in community 8 items: 6, 20*, 21, 36, 37, 52*, 69, 72
8. Acquired Knowledge in a Field 6 items: 8, 23, 70, 65, 63*, 51
9. High School Course Work 5 items: 11, 25, 42, 56, 62*
10. Motivation 6 items: 10, 24*, 40, 55*, 63*, 41
11. Study Method and Effectiveness 7 items: 2, 45*, 12*, 13, 65, 57*, 43*
12. Expectation of Involvement with Faculty 6 items: 20*, 26, 58, 44, 31, 39
13. Emotional Intelligence 7 items: 14, 28, 29, 46, 47, 66, 67

*: reverse scoring
#: items used more than once: 2, 8, 20, 23, 30, 31, 62, 63, 65, 66

Items 1-71: A=5, B=4, C=3, D=2, E=1
Reverse scoring for items 72-78 and 3, 5, 7, 12, 15, 20, 22, 24, 27, 38, 43, 45, 52, 53, 62, 63, 78

Bibliography

Adelman, C. (1999). *Answers in the tool box: Academic intensity, attendance patterns, and bachelor's degree attainment.* Washington, DC: Author.

Allen, T. D., Poteet, M., L. & Burroughs, S. M. (1997). The mentor's perspective: A qualitative inquiry and future research agenda. *Journal of Vocational Behavior, 51(1),* 70-89.

Ancis, J. R., & Sedlacek, W. E. (1997). Predicting the academic achievement of female students using the SAT and noncognitive variables. *College and University, 72(3),* 1-8.

Arbona, C., & Novy, D. M. (1990). Noncognitive dimensions as predictors of college success among Black, Mexico-American, and white students. *Journal of College Student Development, 31,* 415-422.

Armbruster, B. B. (2000). Taking notes from lectures. In R. R. Flippo & D. C. Caverly (Eds.), *Handbook of college reading and strategy research* (pp. 175-199). Mahwah, NJ: Erlbaum.

Association for Specialists in Group Work (2005). *Best practice guidelines.* [online]. Available: http://www.asgw.org/best.

Astin, A. W. (1984). Student involvement: A developmental theory for higher education. *Journal of College Student Personnel, 26(4),* 297-308.

Astin, A. W. (1993). What matters in college. *Liberal Education, 79(4),* 4-15.

Astin, A. W. (1997). *What matters in college? Four critical years revisited.* San Francisco: Jossey-Bass.

Attinasi, L. (1992). Rethinking the study of the outcomes of college attendance. *Journal of College Student Development, 33,* 61-70.

Barefoot, B. O. & Fidler, P. P. (1996). *The 1994 National Survey of freshman Seminar Programs: Continuing innovations in the collegiate curriculum.* Columbia: University of South Carolina, National Resources Center for The First-Year-Experience and Students in Transition.

Baron, J., & Norman, F. (1992). SAT, achievement tests, and high school class rank as predictors of college performance. *Educational and Psychological Measurement, 52,* 1047-1055.

Beal, P. E., & Noel, Lee (1979). *What Works in Student Retention. A Preliminary Summary of a National Survey Conducted Jointly.* Iowa City, IA: The American College Testing Program.

Bennett, C. I. (2002). Enhancing ethnic diversity at a Big Ten university through project TEAM: A case study in teacher education. *Educational Researcher, 31,* 21-29.

Berg, B. L. (2007). *Qualitative research methods for the social sciences.* (6th Ed.). Boston: Pearson/Allyn & Bacon.

Biggs, S., Torres, S., & Washington, N. (1998). Minority student retention: A framework for discussion and decision making. *Negro Educational Review,*

49, 71-82.

Bowen, W. G., & Bok, D. (1998). *The shape of the river: long-term consequences of considering race in college and university admissions.* Princeton, N.J.: Princeton University Press.

Boyer, S. P., & Sedlacek, W. E. (1988). Noncognitive predictors of academic success for international students: A longitudinal study. *Journal of College Student Development, 29*, 218-222.

Braxton, J., Sullivan, A., & Johnson, R. (1997). Appraising Tinto's theory of college student departure. In J. C. Smart (Ed.), *Higher education: Handbook of theory and research* (Vol. 12, pp. 107-158). New York: Agathon.

Burke, R., McKenna, C., & McKenna, C. (1993). Correlates of mentoring in organizations: The mentor's perspective. *Psychological Reports, 72*, 883–896.

Burton, E., & Ramist (2001). *Predicting success in college: SAT studies of classes graduating since 1980 (Research Report 2001-2002).* New York: College Entrance Examination Board.

Carnevale, A. P., & Fry, R. A. (2000). *Crossing the great divide: Can we achieve equity when generation Y goes to college?* Washington, D.C.: Educational Testing Service.

Chao, G. T. (1997). Mentoring Phases and Outcomes. *Journal of Vocational Behavior, 51(1)*, 15-28.

Chickering, A. W. & Reisser, L. (1993). *Education and identity* (2nd ed.). San Francisco: Jossey-Bass.

Chronicle of Higher Education (2002) *The Almanac.* [on-line]. Available: *http://chronicle.com/weekly/almanac/2002/nation/0102302.htm.*

Chronicle of Higher Education Almanac (2005). The Nation: Students. *The Chronicle of Higher Education.* p.14-17.

College Board (1988). *Guidelines on the uses of College Board test scores and related data.* New York: College Entrance Examination Board.

College Board (1996). *The new SAT.* New York: College Entrance Examination Board.

Cooper, D. (1999). Changing the faces of mathematics Ph.D.: What are we learning at the University of Maryland. *Changing the faces of mathematics: Perspectives on African Americans.* National Council of Teachers of Mathematics.

Corey, M. S. , & Corey, G. (2003). *Groups: Process and Practice.* (6th ed.). Pacific Grove: Brooks/Cole.

Cormier, S. & Nurius, P. S. (2003). *Interviewing and change strategies for helpers: Fundamental skills and cognitive behavioral interventions.* (5th ed.). Brooks/Cole: Pacific Grove.

Department of Education (2002). *Digest of Education Statistics, 2001.*

Washington, D.C.: Government Printing Office.

Donigan, J., & Malnati, R. (1997). *Systematic group therapy: A triadic model.* Pacific Grove: Brooks/Cole.

Ender, S., Winston, R. W., & Miller T. (1982). Academic advising as student development. In R. Winston, S. Ender, and T. Miller (Eds.). *New Directions for Student Services: Developmental Approaches to Academic Advising. No. 17.* Jossey-Bass.

Erikson, J. M. (1997). *The life cycle completed.* New York: Norton.

Fagenson-Eland, E. A., Mark, M. A., & Amendola, K. L. (1997). Perceptions of mentoring relationship, *Journal of Vocational Behavior, 51*, 29-42.

Feldman, R. S. (2007). *POWER Learning Strategies for success in college and life.* Boston, MA: McGraw-Hill.

Fleming, J. (1984). *Blacks in college.* San Francisco: Jossey-Bass.

Flippo, R. R., & Caverly, D. C. (Eds.). (2000). *Handbook of college reading and strategy research* (pp. 175-199). Mahwah, NJ: Erlbaum.

Fogleman, B. S., & Saeger, W. (1985). Examining Sedlacek's nontraditional variables of minority student success in a summer enrichment program for health careers. *Journal of the National Medical Association, 78(1),* 545-549.

Forester-Miller, H. (1993). Jack A. Duncan: Twenty years with ASGW. *Journal for Specialists in Group Work, 18(4),* 164-173.

Fuertes, J. N., & Sedlacek, W. E. (1995). Using noncognitive variables to predict the grades and retention of Hispanic students. *College Student Affairs Journal, 14(2),* 30-36.

Fuertes, J. N., Sedlacek, W. E., & Liu, W. M. (1994). Using the SAT and noncognitive variables to predict the grades and retention of Asian American university students. *Measurement and Evaluation in Counseling and Development, 27,* 74-84.

Gardner, H. (1999). *Intelligence reframed: Multiple intelligences for the 21st century.* New York, NY: Basic Books.

Gazda, G. M. (1989). *Group counseling: A developmental approach.* (4th ed.). Boston: Allyn and Bacon.

Gazda, G. M., Horne, A., & Ginter, E. (2001). *Group counseling and group psychotherapy: Theory and application.* Boston: Allyn & Bacon.

Gerald, D. E. (1992). *Projections of education statistics to 2003.* Washington, D.C.: National Center for Education Statistics.

Goldberg, L. R. (2001). *The big-five factor structure as a framework for the consideration of noncognitive assessments for graduate admissions.* Paper presented at Symposium on Noncognitive Assessments for Graduate Admissions, Graduate Record Examination Board, Toronto.

Gordon, V. N. (1989). Origins and purposes of the freshman seminar. In M. L. Upcraft, J. N. Gardner, & Associates (Eds.), *The freshman year experience: Helping students survive and succeed in college* (pp.183-197). San

Francisco: Jossey-Bass.

Gose, B. & Selingo, J. (2001, October 21). The SAT's Greatest Test: Social, legal, and demographic forces threaten to dethrone the most widely used college-entrance exam. *The Chronicle of Higher Education.* [On-line] Available: http://chronicle.com/chronicle/v48/4809guide.htm.

Hebel, S. (2002, November 8). New admissions process at 6 University of California campuses retains academic quality, faculty review says. *Chronicle of Higher Education.*[on-line] http://chronicle.com/daily/2002/11/200211080n.htm.

Helms, J. E. (1995). An update of Helms' white and people of color racial identity models. In J. G. Ponterotto, J. M. Casas, L. A. Suzuki, & C. M. Alexander (Eds.), *Handbook of multicultural counseling* (pp. 181-198). Thousand Oaks, CA: Sage.

Herman, J. & Schatzow, E. (1984). Time-limited group therapy for women with a history of group incest. *Journal of Group Psychotherapy, 36(4),* 605-616.

Hezlett, S.A., Kuncel, N. R., Vey, M., Ahart, A. M., Ones, D. S., Campbell, J. P., & Camara, W. (2001, April). *The effectiveness of the SAT in predicting success early and later in college: A meta-analysis.* Paper presented at the AERA/NCME annual meeting, Seattle, W.A.

Hill, W. (1995). *The academic retention and graduation status of African American students: Factors in a public university.* Doctoral dissertation, North Carolina State University.

Hoey, J. J. (1997). *Developing a retention risk indicator at North Carolina State University.* Raleigh: North Carolina State University.

Hood, D. W. (1992). Academic and noncognitive factors affecting the retention of Black men at a predominantly White university. *Journal of Negro Education, 61,* 12-23.

Houston, L. N. (1980). Predicting academic achievement among specially admitted Black female college students. *Educational and Psychological Measurement, 40,* 1189-1195.

Hunter, M. S., & Linder, C. W. (2005). First-Year Seminars. In M. L. Upcraft, J. N. Gardner, B. O. Barefoot, & Associates (Eds.), *Challenging and supporting the first-year student: A handbook for improving the first year of college.* (pp.275-291). San Francisco: Jossey-Bass.

Johnson-Bailey, J., & Cervero, R. M. (2002). Cross-cultural mentoring as a context for learning. *New Directions for Adult and Continuing Education, 96,* 15-26.

Koberg, C. S., Boss, R. W., & Goodman, E. (1998). Factors and outcomes associated with mentoring among health-care professionals. *Journal of Vocational Behavior, 53(1),* 58-72.

Kuh, G. D., Schuh, J. H., Whitt, E. J., & Associates (1991). *Involving colleges: Successful approaches to fostering learning and development outside the classroom.* San Francisco: Jossey-Bass.

Liu, W. M., & Sedlacek, W. E. (1999). Differences in leadership and co-curricular perception among entering male and female Asian-Pacific-American college students. *Journal of the First-Year Experience and Students in Transition, 11*, 93-114.

Manski, C. F., & Wise, D. A. (1983). *College choice in America.* Cambridge, M.A.: Harvard University Press.

Meichenbaum, D. (1977). *Cognitive behavior modification: An integrative approach.* New Your: Plenum.

Milem, J. F., & Berger, J. B. (1998). A modified model of college student persistence: Exploring the relationship between Astin's Theory of Involvement and Tinto's theory of Student Departure. *Journal of College Student Development, 38,* 387-400.

Mullendore, R. H., & Banahan, L. A. (2005). Designing orientation programs. In M. L. Upcraft, J. N. Gardner, B. O. Barefoot, & Associates (Eds.), *Challenging and supporting the first-year student: A handbook for improving the first year of college.* (pp.391-409). San Francisco: Jossey-Bass.

Mundsack, A., Deese, J., & Deese, E. K. (2002). *How to study.* (5th ed.). New York: McGraw-Hill.

National Center for Fair and Open Testing (2000). *281 Schools that have eliminated or reduced SAT and ACT requirements for admission into bachelor degree programs.* Cambridge, MA: FairTest.

National Resources Center for The First-Year-Experience and Students in Transition (2002). *The 2000 national survey for first-year seminars programs: Continuing innovations in the collegiate curriculum.* Columbia: University of South Carolina, Author.

National Sciences Foundation (2004). *Science and Engineering Degrees by race/ethnicity of recipients 1992-2001.* [On-line]. Available: http://www.ns f. gov/ statistics/nsf04318/pdf/tab1.pdf.

Nisbet, J., Ruble, V. E., & Schurr, K. T. (1982). Predictors of academic success with high risk college students. *Journal of College Student Personnel, 23,* 227-235.

Nora, A., & Cabrera, A. (1996). The role and perception of prejudice and discrimination on the adjustment of minority students to college. *Journal of Higher Education, 67,* 119-148.

Olejnik, S., & Nist, S. L. (1992). Identifying latent variables measured by the Learning and Study Strategies Inventory (LASSI). *Journal of Experimental Education, 60(2),* 151-159.

Pascarella, E. T., & Terenzini, P. T., (2005). *How college affects students.* San Francisco: Jossey-Bass.

Proctor, B. E., Prevatt, F., Adams, K., Hurst, A., & Petscher, Y. (2006). Study skills profiles of normal-achieving and academically-struggling college students, *Journal of College Student Development, 47 (1),* 37-51.

Ragins, R. R., & McFarin, D. B. (1990). Perceptions of mentor roles in cross-gender mentoring relationships. *Journal of Vocational Behavior, 37(3),*

321-329.

Rose, S. D. (1989). *Working with adults in groups: Integrating cognitive-behavioral and small group strategies.* San Francisco: Jossey-Bass

Scandura, T. A. (1992). Mentorship and career mobility: An empirical investigation. *Journal of Organizational Behavior, 13,* 169–174.

Sedlacek, W. E. (1987). Black students on White campuses: 20 years of research. *Journal of College Student Development, 27,* 484-495.

Sedlacek, W. E. (1991). Using noncognitive variables in advising nontraditional students. *The Journal of the National Academic Advising Association, 11,* 75-82.

Sedlacek, W. E. (1996) An empirical method of determining nontraditional group status. *Measurement and Evaluation in Counseling and Development, 28,* 200-210.

Sedlacek, W. E. (1998). Multiple choices for standardized tests. *Priorities, 10,* Winter, 1-15.

Sedlacek, W. E. (2003). Alternative measures in admissions and scholarship selection. *Measurement and Evaluation in Counseling and Development, 35,* 263-272.

Sedlacek, W. E. (2004). *Beyond the big test: Noncognitive assessment in higher education.* San Francisco: Jossey-Bass.

Sedlacek, W. E. (2007). *Dr. Sedlacek's publications, articles, surveys.* [On-line]. Available: http://www.williamsedlacek.info/publications/articles/profiles1.html.

Sedlacek, W. E., & Adams-Gaston, J. (1992). Predicting the academic success of student-athletes using SAT and noncognitive variables. *Journal of Counseling and Development, 70 (6),* 24-27.

Sedlacek, W. E., & Brooks, G. C., Jr. (1976). *Racism in American education: A model for change.* Chicago: Nelson-Hall.

Seidman, I. (2006). *Interviewing as qualitative research: A guide for researchers in education and the social sciences.* (3rd ed.). New York : Teachers College Press.

Shaffer, J. B. P., & Galinsky, M. D. (1989). *Models of group therapy.* (2nd ed.). New Jersey: Prentice Hall.

Sowa, C. J., Thomson, M. M., & Bennett, C. T. (1989). Prediction and improvement of academic performance for high- risk black college students. *Journal of Multicultural Counseling and Development, 17,* 14-21.

Sternberg, R. J. (1985). *Beyond I.Q.* London: Cambridge.

Sternberg, R. J. (1993). The concept of intelligence and its role in lifelong learning and success. *American Psychologist, 52 (10),* 1030-1037.

Sternberg, R. J. (1996). *Successful intelligence.* New York: Plume.

Stonehouse, C., & Ting, S. R. (2000). Effects of a structured group intervention on academic achievement and retention of First Year College student. *North*

Carolina Journal of College Student Development, 1, 3-9.

Tierney, W. (1992). An anthropological analysis of student participation in college. *Journal of Higher Education. 63,* 603-618.

Ting, S. R. (1997a). Estimating academic success in the First year of college for specially admitted White students: A model of combining cognitive and psychosocial predictors. *Journal of College Student Development, 38,* 401-409.

Ting, S. R. (1997b). Excellence-Commitment-and-Effective-Learning Group (ExCEL): An intervention program for academically high-risk students. *The National Academic Advising Association (NACADA) Journal, 17 (2),* Fall, 48-51.

Ting, S. R. (1998). Predicting first-year grades and retention of college students of first-generation and low-income families. *Journal of College Admissions, 158, Winter,* 14-23.

Ting, S. R. (1999). *Academic performance and student retention of students enrolled in University Transition Program.* Raleigh, North Carolina State University.

Ting, S. R. (2000a). Predicting Asian Americans' academic performance in the first year of college: An approach combining SAT scores and noncognitive variables. *Journal of College Student Development, 41,* 442-449.

Ting, S. R. (2000b). *Predicting academic performance and retention of college students using SAT scores, high school GPA and noncognitive variables: 4 years later.* Raleigh, NC: NC State University, Department of Educational Research and Leadership and Counselor Education.

Ting, S. R. (2000c). *Exploring the impact of psychosocial variables on academic performance and retention of student athletes in the first year of college.* Raleigh, NC: North Carolina State University, Office of Academic Support for Student Athletes.

Ting, S. R. (2001). Predicting academic success of first-year engineering students from standardized test scores and psychosocial variables. *International Journal for Engineering Education, 17(1),* 75-80.

Ting, S. R., & Bryant, A., Jr. (2001). The impact of acculturation and psychosocial variables on academic performance of Native American and Caucasian Freshmen. *Journal of College Admission, 171, Spring,* 22-28.

Ting, S. R., Grant, S., & Plenert, S. (2000). An application of repeated structured groups enhancing college first-year students' success. *Journal of College Student Development, 41,* 353-360.

Ting, S. R. & Robinson, T. L. (1998). First-year academic success: A prediction combining cognitive and psychosocial variables for Caucasian and African American students. *Journal of College Student Development, 39,* 599-610.

Ting, S. R. & Sedlacek, W. E. (2000, March). The validity of the Non-Cognitive *Questionnaire-Revised 2 in predicting academic success of university freshmen.* Paper presented at the Annual Convention of American College

Personnel Association, Washington, D.C.

Tinto. V. (1973). Dropouts from higher education: A theoretical synthesis of recent research. *Review of Educational Research, 45,* 89-125.

Tinto, V. (1989). Theories of college student departure revisited. In J. C. Smart (Ed.), *Higher education handbook of theory and research, Vol. 2,* (pp.359-384). New York: Agathon Press.

Tinto, V. (1993). *Leaving college: Rethinking the causes and cures of student attrition* (2nd ed.). Chicago: University of Chicago Press.

Tracey, T. J., & Sedlacek, W. E. (1984). Noncognitive variables in predicting academic success by race. *Measurement and Evaluation in Guidance, 16,* 171-178.

Tracey, T. J., & Sedlacek, W. E. (1985). The relationship of noncognitive variables to academic success: A longitudinal comparison by race. *Journal of College Student Personnel, 26,* 410.

Tracey, T. J., & Sedlacek, W. E (1987). Predicting college graduation using noncognitive variables by race. *Measurement and Evaluation in Counseling and Development, 19,* 177-184.

Tracey T. J., & Sedlacek, W. E. (1988). A comparison of White and Black student academic success using noncognitive variables: A LISERL analysis. *Research in Higher Education, 27,* 333-348.

Tracey, T. J., & Sedlacek, W. E. (1989). Factor structure of the noncognitive questionnaire: Revised across samples of Black and White college students. *Educational and Psychological Measurements, 49,* 637-648.

University of Berkeley (2003). *Freshman Admission brochure* [on-line] Available: http://admissions.berkeley.edu/pdf/Fresh.pdf.

Upcraft, L. (2005). Assessing the first year college. In M. L. Upcraft, J. N. Gardner, B. O. Barefoot, & Associates (Eds.), *Challenging and supporting the first-year student: A handbook for improving the first year of college.* (pp.469-485). San Francisco: Jossey-Bass.

Watkins, D. (1986). Learning processes and background characteristics as predictors of tertiary grades. *Educational and Psychological Measurement, 46,* 199-203.

Wawrzynski, M. R., & Sedlacek, w. E. (2003, March). *Using Noncognitive variables as a new assessment method.* American College Personnel Association annual meeting, Minneapolis, MN.

Weinstein, C. E., & Palmer, D. R. (1987). *Learning and Study Strategies Inventory.* Clear Water, FL: H & H.

Wells. E., & Knefelkamp, L. (1984). *Workbook for the Practice-to-Theory-to-Practice Model.* University of Maryland-College Park.

Westbrook, F. D., & Sedlacek, W. E. (1991). Forty years of using labels to communicate about nontraditional students: does it help or hurt? *Journal of Counseling and Development, 70,* 20-28.

White, T. J., & Sedlacek, W. E. (1986). Noncognitive predictors: Grades and retention of specially admitted students. *Journal of College Admissions, 3, Spring,* 20-23.

Wilds, D. (2000). *Minorities in higher education 1999-2000: Seventeenth Annual Status Report.* Washington, D. C.: American Council on Education.

Williams, R. L., & Worth, S. L. (2002). Thinking skills and work habits: Contributors to course performance. *The Journal of General Education, 51(3),* 200-227.

Winston, R. B., Jr., Bonney, W. C., Miller, T. K., & Dagley, J. C. (1988). *Promoting student development through intentionally structured groups: Principles, techniques, and applications.* San Francisco: Jossey-Bass.

Wright, D. (1987). *Responding to the needs of today's college students.* San Francisco: Jossey-Bass.

Yalom, I. D., & Leszcz, M. (2005). *The theory and practice of group psychotherapy.* (5th ed.). New York: Basic Books.

Zwick, R. (2002). *Fair game: The use of standardized admissions tests in higher education.* New York: RoutledgeFalmer.

Subject Index

A
A strong support person, 9, 10, 19, 29, 39, 77, 81
Academic achievement, 3, 4, 19, 30
Academic advising, 14, 17, 37
Academic preparation, 3
Academic seminars, 15
Academic support program(s), 68, 77
African American(s), 1, 2, 4, 11, 59, 73, 75, 76, 82, 83
Asian Americans, 11, 36, 41, 72
Assessment, 5, 12, 19, 21, 28, 29, 33, 34, 39, 80, 81, 82
Association for Specialist in Group Work, 29
Attrition, 2, 3, 10, 36

B
Best Practice Guidelines in Group Work, 29

C
Campus activities, 5
Caucasians, 1, 10, 11, 21, 26, 41, 62, 68, 72, 73, 75, 76, 81
Chronicle of Higher Education, 1, 23
Class size, 14, 38
Coaching, 63
Cognitive behavioral strategies, 25
Commitment, 5, 6, 34, 37, 53, 76
Control group, 30, 37, 38, 71-76, 80
Counselors, 17, 61, 62, 76-78
Curriculum, 14, 15, 38

D
Demonstrated community service, 9, 10, 19, 39, 41, 44
Depression, 29
Developmental structured group, 19
Disabilities, 36, 83
Diversity, 3, 15, 18, 23, 62, 77
Dropping out, 1, 30, 70, 71, 75

E
Effective Study Skills Test, 47
Empirical research, 33
Enrollment, 1, 2, 4, 11, 19, 30, 42, 70, 71, 73, 74, 82
Ethical issues, 29, 31
Evaluation, program, 37
Exit interview(s), 20, 67, 69
Expectation, college, 7
Expectations, academic, 23

F
Feedback, 9, 22, 25, 27, 28, 34, 40, 43, 52, 56, 63, 68
Financial aid, 4, 23, 44, 81, 82
First generation college students, 20
First Year College, 17, 37, 75
First-year experience, 16
First-year seminar, 13-16, 34, 36-38, 77, 83
Freshman seminar, 74

G
Grade-point-average, 10, 37, 64, 67, 70, 71
GPAs, 2, 4, 11, 30, 38, 70-75, 77, 82
Graduation rate, 11, 82
Ground rules, 47, 48, 62
Group,

dynamics, 31
forming, 30
goals, 9, 23, 24
members, 33
norms, 22
process, 22, 24, 29, 31, 32, 34, 66, 72, 76, 80, 83
rules, 27, 47
size, 77, 78
termination of, 66
topics, 47, 68
Group work, 21, 22, 29, 67, 79, 83
Guided imagery, 25, 26, 57

H

High risk students, 80
High school grades, 82
High School GPA, 2, 3, 38, 73-75
Hispanics, 1, 3, 11, 21, 41, 59, 75
Hmongs, 36

I

Imagery, 25, 26, 28, 57
Intellectual development, 6
International students, 11, 18, 21, 59, 69
Interviews, 34, 67, 71, 75
Involvement,
    in college life, 8
    in community, 10, 55
    in student activities, 23, 64, 65, 77
    with faculty, 45, 46

J

Job, part-time, 36, 50
Jobs, how to find, 60

K

Knowledge acquired in a field, 8, 10, 11, 39, 44

L

Learning and Study Strategies

    Inventory, 30, 47, 48, 49, 67, 71-75.
Learning communities, 14, 16
Learning experiences, 5, 17, 77
Low-income students, 11, 36
Living in a multicultural society, 27, 35, 43, 62, 63

M

Memory, 35, 47, 51-53
Mentors, 4, 13, 16, 41, 61, 62
Minority students, 2, 3, 64
Mnemonics, 53
Model, role, 4, 13, 26, 27, 83
Modeling, 25, 26
Motivation, 3, 7, 8, 30, 39, 45-47, 67, 69, 83
Multicultural diversity, 23
Myers-Briggs Types Indicators, 47

N

National Resources Center for First-Year Experiences and Students in Transition, 14
National Survey of First Year Seminar Programming, 15
Non-Cognitive,
    assessment, 29, 39
    Questionnaire, 10, 13, 19, 21, 31, 39, 67, 79, 82
    Questionnaire-Revised Two, 45
    Variables, 5, 6, 8, 11, 19, 21, 39-42, 44, 68-71, 77, 81, 83
Non-traditional students, 13, 21, 33, 77, 79, 80

North Carolina State University, 11, 15, 17, 36-37, 42, 73, 80

O
Older students, 13, 33
Orientation, student, 14, 24, 36, 42

P
Part-time students, 23,
Peer group, 5, 6, 61
Persistence, 4, 5, 6, 22, 45
Positive self-concept, 8, 10, 11, 19, 39, 57
Preference of long-range goals, 10, 19
Principles of Good Practice, 81

Q
Qualitative approach, 67, 71
Questions, open-ended, 27, 55, 56, 67, 71

R
Race/ethnicity, 1, 4, 6, 38, 43, 68, 71, 73, 75, 76
Racial identity development, 26
Realistic self-appraisal, 8, 10, 19, 27, 39, 55, 56, 40
Recruitment, of students, 33, 72, 79
Reframing, 25, 27, 55
Renewed Commitment Program, 37, 76
Residence halls, 14, 17, 36, 37, 50, 73, 80
Retention, 1, 4-6, 11, 13, 21, 30, 34, 41, 67, 71-77
Role-play(s) (ing), 23, 25, 27, 62, 63

S
Screening of group members, 14, 29
Self-concept, 20, 23, 26, 55, 57, 59, 69, 77, 81

Self-management, 25, 28
Small groups, 16, 21, 22, 30, 77, 80
Specially-admitted students, 11
Standardized tests, 5, 8, 39
Structured group, 19, 24, 33, 37
Student affairs, 36, 81
Student affairs professionals, 14-16, 61, 62, 64, 78
Student departure model, 5,
Student development, 4, 13, 16, 20, 31, 37, 68
Student involvement, 5
Student learning, 81
Study groups, 83
Study skills, 14, 15, 18, 19, 21, 23, 30, 31, 34-36, 38, 46-49, 51, 67, 76, 77, 80, 81
Successful leadership experience, 9, 10, 39, 44, 64
Supplemental instruction, 14
Support group, 16, 34, 66, 79
Systematic desensitization, 25, 28

T
Test taking, 23, 75
Themes (of group sessions), 35
Time management, 28, 30, 35, 38, 47, 49-51, 67, 75
Training, 4, 21, 22, 24, 25, 28, 30, 31, 34, 38
Training approach, 25
Treatment group, 30, 37, 72-76
Trio Program, 34, 36, 72-73, 77
Trust, 30

U
University of Wisconsin-River Falls, 34, 72, 80
University Transition Program, 37, 74, 77, 80

V

Voluntary participation, 13, 29

W

Women, 13, 18, 25, 27, 33, 59, 62, 63

Y

Youth, 1

About the Author

Dr. S. Raymond Ting, LPC NCC CDFI is Associate Professor, Assistant Department Head and Director of Counselor Education Graduate Program of the Department of Curriculum and Instruction at North Carolina State University. He also coordinates the college counseling track of the Counselor Education program. He completed his doctoral degree in Counselor Education from the University of Iowa, with a concentration in student development in higher education in 1995. Dr. Ting is a national scholar in college student development and international application in career development. He has published extensively on academic performance and student retention in many professional journals. He developed the Chinese Career Key website [http://www.careerkey.org/Chinese] in 2001 which has been popular in Hong Kong and China. At present, he is the lead principal investigator for a three-year project on science enrichment and career development sponsored by the Burroughs Wellcome Fund. He has served on several editorial boards of professional journals and as an ad hoc reviewer for international journals in college counseling and college student development such as the *Journal of College Student Development and Journal of College Counseling*. At present, he coordinates the international collaboration committee for the American College Counseling Association and is the President of the North Carolina College Counseling Association. He has received many professional awards, including the Ralph Berdie Memorial Research Award from the American Counseling Association, and Annuit Copetis Award from the American College Personnel Association.

www.ingramcontent.com/pod-product-compliance
Lightning Source LLC
Chambersburg PA
CBHW021834300426
44114CB00009BA/436